STANTON'S REPORTER

CHARLES A. DANA IN THE CIVIL WAR

BY

CHARLES A. DANA

ASSISTANT SECRETARY of WAR FROM 1863 TO 1868

Originally published as *Recollections of the Civil War*

1898

COPYRIGHT 2018

DISCOVER MORE LOST HISTORY AT BIGBYTEBOOKS.COM

Contents

PREFACE	1
FROM THE *TRIBUNE* TO THE WAR DEPARTMENT	3
AT THE FRONT WITH GRANT'S ARMY	15
BEFORE AND AROUND VICKSBURG	29
IN CAMP AND BATTLE WITH GRANT AND HIS GENERALS	38
SOME CONTEMPORARY PORTRAITS	48
THE SIEGE OF VICKSBURG	64
PEMBERTON'S SURRENDER	74
WITH THE ARMY OF THE CUMBERLAND	83
THE REMOVAL OF ROSECRANS	96
CHATTANOOGA AND MISSIONARY RIDGE	105
THE WAR DEPARTMENT IN WAR TIMES	123
ABRAHAM LINCOLN AND HIS CABINET	132
THE ARMY OF THE POTOMAC IN '64	146
THE GREAT GAME BETWEEN GRANT AND LEE	157
THE MARCH ON PETERSBURG	165
EARLY'S RAID AND THE WASHINGTON PANIC	174
THE SECRET SERVICE OF THE WAR.	182
A VISIT TO SHERIDAN IN THE VALLEY	191
"ON TO RICHMOND" AT LAST!	203
THE CLOSING SCENES AT WASHINGTON	210

PREFACE

The late Charles A. Dana's "Recollections of the Civil War" forms one of the most remarkable volumes of historical, political, and personal reminiscences which have been given to the public. Mr. Dana was not only practically a member of the Cabinet and in the confidence of the leaders of Washington, but he was also the chosen representative of the War Department with General Grant and other military commanders, and he was present at many of the councils which preceded movements of the greatest importance.

Mr. Dana wrote these Recollections of the civil war according to a purpose which he had entertained for several years. They were completed only a few months before his death on October 17, 1897. A large part of the narrative has been published serially in *McClure's Magazine.* In the chapter about Abraham Lincoln and the Lincoln Cabinet Mr. Dana has drawn from a lecture which he delivered in 1896 before the New Haven Colony Historical Society. The incident of the self-wounded spy, in the chapter relating to the secret service of the war, was first printed in the *North American Review* for August, 1891. A few of the anecdotes about Mr. Lincoln which appear in this book were told by Mr. Dana originally in a brief contribution to a volume entitled *Reminiscences of Abraham Lincoln by Distinguished Men of his Time*, edited by the late Allen Thorndike Rice, and published in 1886.

Although Mr. Dana was in one sense the least reminiscent of men, living actively in the present, and always more interested in tomorrow than in yesterday, and although it was his characteristic habit to toss into the wastebasket documents for history which many persons would have treasured, he found in the preparation of the following chapters abundant material wherewith to stimulate and confirm his own memory, in the form of his official and unofficial reports written at the front for the information of Mr. Stanton and Mr. Lincoln, and private letters to members of his family and intimate friends.

Charles Anderson Dana was forty-four years old when his appointment as Assistant Secretary of War put him behind the scenes of the great drama then enacting, and brought him into personal relations with the conspicuous civilians and soldiers of the war period. Born in New Hampshire on August 8, 1819, he had passed by way of western New York, Harvard College, and Brook Farm into the profession which he loved and in which he labored almost to the last day of his life. When Secretary Stanton called him to Washington he had been engaged for nearly fifteen years in the management of the New York *Tribune*, the journal most powerful at that time in solidifying Northern sentiment for the crisis that was to come. When the war was over and the Union preserved, he returned at once to journalism. His career subsequently as the editor of *The Sun* for thirty years is familiar to most Americans.

It is proper to note the circumstance that the three years covered by Mr. Dana's Recollections as here recorded constitute the only term during which he held any public office, and the only break in more than half a century of continuous experience in the making of newspapers. His connection with the Government during those momentous years is an episode in the story of a life that throbbed from boyhood to age with intellectual energy, and was crowded with practical achievement.

New York, October 17, 1898.

FROM THE *TRIBUNE* TO THE WAR DEPARTMENT

I had been associated with Horace Greeley on the New York *Tribune* for about fifteen years when, one morning early in April, 1862, Mr. Sinclair, the advertising manager of the paper, came to me, saying that Mr. Greeley would be glad to have me resign. I asked one of my associates to find from Mr. Greeley if that was really his wish. In a few hours he came to me saying that I had better go. I stayed the day out in order to make up the paper and give them an opportunity to find a successor, but I never went into the office after that. I think I then owned a fifth of the paper—twenty shares; this stock my colleagues bought.

Mr. Greeley never gave a reason for dismissing me, nor did I ever ask for one. I know, though, that the real explanation was that while he was for peace I was for war, and that as long as I stayed on the *Tribune* there was a spirit there which was not his spirit—that he did not like.

My retirement from the *Tribune* was talked of in the newspapers for a day or two, and brought me a letter from the Secretary of War, Edwin M. Stanton, saying he would like to employ me in the War Department.

I had already met Mr. Lincoln, and had carried on a brief correspondence with Mr. Stanton. My meeting with Mr. Lincoln was shortly after his inauguration. He had appointed Mr. [William] Seward to be his Secretary of State, and some of the Republican leaders of New York who had been instrumental in preventing Mr. Seward's nomination to the presidency, and in securing that of Mr. Lincoln, had begun to fear that they would be left out in the cold in the distribution of the offices. General James S. Wadsworth, George Opdyke, Lucius Robinson, T. B. Carroll, and Henry B. Stanton were among the number of these gentlemen. Their apprehensions were somewhat mitigated by the fact that Mr. [Salmon] Chase, to whom we were all friendly, was Secretary of the Treasury. But, notwithstanding, they were afraid that the superior tact and pertinacity of Mr. Seward and of Mr. Thurlow Weed, Seward's close friend and political manager, would get the upper hand, and that the power of the Federal administration would be put into the control of the rival faction; accordingly, several of them determined to go to Washington, and I was asked to go with them.

I believe the appointment for our interview with the President was made through Mr. Chase; but at any rate we all went up to the White House together, except Mr. Henry B. Stanton, who stayed away because he was himself an applicant for office.

Mr. Lincoln received us in the large room upstairs in the east wing of the White House, where he had his working office. The President stood up while General Wadsworth, who was our principal spokesman, and Mr. Opdyke stated what was desired. After the interview had begun, a big Indianian, who was a messenger in attendance in the White House, came into the room and said to the President:

"She wants you."

"Yes, yes," said Mr. Lincoln, without stirring. Soon afterward the messenger returned again, exclaiming, "I say, she wants you!"

The President was evidently annoyed, but instead of going out after the messenger he remarked to us:

"One side shall not gobble up everything. Make out a list of places and men you want, and I will endeavor to apply the rule of give and take."

General Wadsworth answered:

"Our party will not be able to remain in Washington, but we will leave such a list with Mr. Carroll, and whatever he agrees to will be agreeable to us."

Mr. Lincoln continued: "Let Mr. Carroll come in tomorrow, and we will see what can be done."

This is the substance of the interview, and what most impressed me was the evident fairness of the President. We all felt that he meant to do what was right and square in the matter. While he was not the man to promote factious quarrels and difficulties within his party, he did not intend to leave in the lurch the friends through whose exertions his nomination and election had finally been brought about. At the same time he understood perfectly that we of New York and our associates in the Republican body had not gone to Chicago for the purpose of nominating him, or of nominating any one in particular, but only to beat Mr. Seward, and thereupon to do the best that could be done as regards the selection of the candidate.

My acquaintance with Mr. Stanton had come about through an editorial which I had written for the *Tribune* on his entrance to the War Department. I had sent it to him with a letter calling his attention to certain facts with which it seemed to me the War Department ought to deal. In reply I received the following letter:

Washington, January 24, 1862.

My dear Sir: Yours of the 22d only reached me this evening. The facts you mention were new to me, but there is too much reason to fear they are true. But that matter will, I think, be corrected very speedily.

You cannot tell how much obligation I feel myself under for your kindness. Every man who wishes the country to pass through this trying hour should stand on watch, and aid me. Bad passions and little passions and mean passions gather around and hem in the great movements that should deliver this nation.

Two days ago I wrote you a long letter—a three pager—expressing my thanks for your admirable article of the 21st, stating my position and purposes; and in that letter I mentioned some of the circumstances of my unexpected appointment. But, interrupted before it was completed, I will not inflict, or afflict, you with it.

I know the task that is before us—I say us, because the *Tribune* has its mission as plainly as I have mine, and they tend to the same end. But I am not in the smallest degree dismayed or disheartened. By God's blessing we shall prevail. I feel a deep, earnest feeling growing up around me. We have no jokes or trivialities, but all with whom I act show that they are now in dead earnest.

I know you will rejoice to know this.

As soon as I can get the machinery of the office working, the rats cleared out, and the rat holes stopped we shall move. This army has got to fight or run away; and while men are striving nobly in the West, the champagne and oysters on the Potomac must be stopped. But patience for a short while only is all I ask, if you and others like you will rally around me.

Yours truly,

Edwin M. Stanton.

A few days after this I wrote Mr. Stanton a second letter, in which I asked him to give General Frémont a chance.

John C. Frémont (1813 – 1890) was a U.S. General known as The Pathfinder for his early explorations of the west. He was a veteran of the Mexican-American War. His wife, Jessie Benton Frémont (1824 – 1902), daughter of Senator Thomas Hart Benton, was a well-known author and early advocate for the preservation of Yosemite Valley as a national park.—Ed. 2018

At the breaking out of the war Frémont had been made a major general in the regular army and the command of the Western Department had been given to him. His campaign in Missouri in the summer of 1861 gave great dissatisfaction, and in November, 1861, he was relieved, after an investigation by the Secretary of War. Since that time he had been without a command. I believed, as did many others, that political intrigue was keeping Frémont back. I was anxious that he should have fair play, in order that the great mass of people who had supported him for the presidency in 1856, and who still were his warm friends, might not be dissatisfied. To my letter Mr. Stanton replied:

Washington, February 1, 1862.

Dear Sir: If General Frémont has any fight in him, he shall (so far as I am concerned) have a chance to show it, and I have told him so. The times require the help of every man according to his gifts, and, having neither partialities nor grudges to indulge, it will be my aim to practice on the maxim, "the tools to him that can handle them."

There will be serious trouble between Hunter and Lane. What Lane's expedition has in view, how it came to be set on foot, and what is expected to be accomplished by it, I do not know and have tried in vain to find out. It seems to be a haphazard affair that no one will admit himself to be responsible for. But believing that Lane has pluck, and is an earnest man, he shall have fair play. If you know anything about him or his expedition pray tell it to me.

To bring the War Department up to the standard of the times, and work an army of five hundred thousand with machinery adapted to a peace establishment of twelve thousand, is no easy task. This was Mr. Cameron's great trouble, and the cause of much of the complaints against him. All I ask is reasonable time and patience. The pressure of members of Congress for clerk and army appointments, notwithstanding the most stringent rules, and the persistent strain against all measures essential to obtain time for thought, combination, and conference, is discouraging in the extreme—it often tempts me to quit the helm in despair. The only consolation is the confidence and support of good and patriotic men; to their aid I look for strength.

Yours truly,

Edwin M. Stanton.

Very soon after Mr. Stanton went into office military affairs were energized, and a forward movement of the armies was apparent. It was followed by several victories, notably those of Fort Henry [February 6, 1862] and Fort Donelson [on February 16, 1862, making Ulysses S. Grant a household name]. On several occasions the *Tribune* credited to the head of the War Department this new spirit which seemed to inspire officers and men. Mr. Stanton, fearful of the effect of this praise, sent to the paper the following dispatch:

To the Editor of the New York *Tribune* :

Sir: I can not suffer undue merit to be ascribed to my official action. The glory of our recent victories belongs to the gallant officers and soldiers that fought the battles. No share of it belongs to me.

Much has recently been said of military combinations and organizing victory. I hear such phrases with apprehension. They commenced in infidel France with the Italian campaign, and resulted in Waterloo. Who can organize victory? Who can combine the elements of success on the battlefield? We owe our recent victories to the spirit of the Lord that moved our soldiers to rush into battle and filled the heart of our enemies with dismay. The inspiration that conquered in battle was in the hearts of the soldiers and from on high; and wherever there is the same inspiration there will be the same results. Patriotic spirit, with resolute courage in officers and men, is a military combination that never failed.

We may well rejoice at the recent victories, for they teach us that battles are to be won now and by us in the same and only manner that they were ever won by any people, or in any age, since the days of Joshua, by boldly pursuing and striking the foe. What, under the blessing of Providence, I conceive to be the true organization of victory and military combination to end this war, was declared in a few words by General Grant's message to General Buckner: "I propose to move immediately on your works."

Yours truly,

Edwin M. Stanton.

On receiving this I at once wired to our representative in Washington to know if Mr. Stanton meant to "repudiate" the *Tribune*. I received my answer from Mr. Stanton himself:

Washington, February 19, 1862.

Dear Sir: It occurred to me that your kind notice of myself might be perverted into a disparagement of the Western officers and soldiers to whom the merit of the recent victories justly belongs, and that it might create an antagonism between them and the head of the War Department. To avoid that misconstruction was the object of my dispatch—leaving the matter to be determined as to publication to the better judgment of the *Tribune*, my own mind not being clear on the point of its expediency. Mr. Hill called to see me this evening, and from the tenor of your dispatch it seemed to me that your judgment did not approve the publication, or you would not speak of me as "repudiating" anything the *Tribune* says. On reflection I am convinced the communication should not be published, as it might imply an antagonism between myself and the *Tribune*. On this, as on any future occasion, I defer to your judgment. We have one heart and mind in this great cause, and upon many essential points you have a wider range of observation and clearer sight than myself; I am therefore willing to be guided by your wisdom.

Yours truly,

Edwin M. Stanton.

On receiving this letter we of course published his telegram at once.

When Mr. Stanton went into the War Department there was great dissatisfaction in the *Tribune* office with [Union General George Brinton] McClellan. He had been placed in command of the Army of the Potomac in the preceding August, and since November 1st had been in command of all the armies of the United States; but while he had proved himself an excellent drillmaster, he had at the same time proved that he was no general at all. His friends were loyal, however, and whatever success our armies met with was attributed to his generalship.

When the capture of Fort Donelson was announced, McClellan's friends claimed that he had directed it by telegraph from his headquarters on the Potomac. Now the terminus of the telegraph toward Fort Donelson was many miles from the battlefield. Besides, the absurdity of a general directing the movements of a battle a thousand miles off, even if he had fifty telegraph wires leading to every part of the field, was apparent. Nevertheless, McClellan's supporters kept up their claim. On February 20th the Associated Press agent at Washington, in reporting a railroad convention in Washington at which Mr. Stanton had spoken, said:

"Secretary Stanton in the course of his address paid a high compliment to the young and gallant friend at his side, Major-General McClellan, in whom he had the utmost confidence, and the results of whose military schemes, gigantic and well matured, were now exhibited to a rejoicing country. The Secretary, with upraised hands, implored Almighty God to aid them and himself, and all occupying positions under the Government, in crushing out this unholy rebellion."

I did not believe Stanton had done any such thing, so I sent the paragraph to him. The Secretary replied:

Washington, February 23, 1862

Dear Sir: The paragraph to which you called my attention was a ridiculous and impudently impertinent effort to puff the general by a false publication of words I never uttered. Sam Barlow, one of the secretaries of the meeting, was its author, as I have been informed.

Barlow was a Democrat and a major stakeholder in the newspaper The New York World.—*Ed. 2018*

It is too small a matter for me to contradict, but I told Mr. Kimlen, the other secretary, that I thought the gentlemen who invited me to be present at their meeting owed it to themselves to see that one of their own officers should not misrepresent what I said. It was for them, and due to their own honor, to see that an officer of the Government might communicate with them in safety; and if it was not done, I should take care to afford no other opportunity for such practices.

The fact is that the agents of the Associated Press and a gang around the Federal Capitol appear to be organized for the purpose of magnifying their idol.

And if such men as those who composed the railroad convention in this city do not rebuke such a practice as that perpetrated in this instance, they cannot be conferred with in future.

You will of course see the propriety of my not noticing the matter and thereby giving it importance beyond the contempt it inspires. I think you are well enough acquainted with me to judge in future the value of any such statement.

I notice the *Herald* telegraphic reporter announces that I had a second attack of illness on Friday and could not attend the department. I was in the department, or in the Cabinet, from nine in the morning until nine at night, and never enjoyed more perfect health than on that day and at present.

For your kind solicitude accept my thanks. I shall not needlessly impair my means of usefulness.

Yours truly,

Edwin M. Stanton.

P. S.—Was It not a funny sight to see a certain military hero in the telegraph office at Washington last Sunday organizing victory, and by sublime military combinations capturing Fort Donelson six hours after Grant and Smith had taken it sword in hand and had victorious possession! It would be a picture worthy of *Punch*.

Thus, when the newspapers announced my unexpected retirement from the *Tribune*, I was not unknown to either the President or the Secretary of War.

To Mr. Stanton's letter asking me to go into the service of the War Department, I replied that I would attempt anything he wanted me to do, and in May he wrote me that I was to be appointed on a commission to audit unsettled claims against the quartermaster's department at Cairo, Ill. I was directed to be in Cairo on June 17th. My formal appointment, which I did not receive until after I reached Cairo, read thus:

War Department, Washington City, D. C.,

June 16, 1862.

Sir: By direction of the President, a commission has been appointed, consisting of Messrs. George S. Boutwell, Stephen T. Logan, and yourself, to examine and report upon all unsettled claims against the War Department, at Cairo, Ill., that may have originated prior to the first day of April, 1862.

Messrs. Boutwell and Logan have been requested to meet with you at Cairo on the eighteenth day of June instant, in order that the commission may be organized on that day and enter immediately upon the discharge of its duties.

You will be allowed a compensation of eight dollars per day and mileage.

Mr. Thomas Means, who has been appointed solicitor for the Government, has been directed to meet you at Cairo on the eighteenth instant, and will act, under the direction of the commission, in the investigation of such claims as may be presented.

Edwin M. Stanton,

Secretary of War.

On reaching Cairo on the appointed day, I found my associates, Judge Logan, of Springfield, Ill., one of Mr. Lincoln's friends, and

Mr. Boutwell, of Massachusetts, afterward Governor of his State, Secretary of the Treasury, and a United States senator. We organized on the 18th, as directed. Two days after we met Judge Logan was compelled by illness to resign from the commission, and Shelby M. Cullom, now United States senator from Illinois, was appointed in his place.

The main Union armies had by this time advanced far to the front, but Cairo was still an important military depot, almost an outpost, in command of General William K. Strong, whom I had known well in New York as a politician. There was a large number of troops stationed in the town, and from there the armies on the Mississippi River, in Missouri, and in Kentucky, got all their supplies and munitions of war. The quartermaster's department at Cairo had been organized hastily, and the demands upon it had increased rapidly. Much of the business had been done by green volunteer officers who did not understand the technical duties of making out military requisitions and returns. The result was that the accounts were in great confusion, and hysterical newspapers were charging the department with fraud and corruption. The War Department decided to make a full investigation of all disbursements at Cairo from the beginning. Little actual cash had thus far been paid out upon contracts, and it was not too late to correct overcharges and straighten out the system. The matter could not be settled by any ordinary means, and the commission went there as a kind of supreme authority, accepting or rejecting claims and paying them as we thought fit after examining the evidence.

Sixteen hundred and ninety-six claims, amounting to $599,219.36 [$14,267,127.62 in 2015], were examined by us. Of those approved and certified for payment the amount was $451,105.80. Of the claims rejected, a considerable portion were for losses suffered in the active operations of the army, either through departure from discipline on the part of soldiers, or from requisitions made by officers who failed to give receipts and certificates to the persons concerned, who were thus unable to support their claims by sufficient evidence. Many claims of this description were also presented by men whose loyalty to the Government was impeached by credible witnesses. In rejecting these, the commission set forth the disloyalty of the claimants, in the certificates written on the face of their accounts. Other accounts, whose rightfulness was established, were rejected on proof of disloyalty. The commission regarded complicity in the rebellion as barring all claims against the United States.

A question of some interest was raised by the claim of the trustees of the Cairo city property to be paid for .the use by the Government wharf boats of the paved portion of the levee which protected the town against the Ohio River. We were unable to see the matter in the light presented by the trustees. Our judgment was that the Government ought not to pay for the use of necessary landing places on these rivers or elsewhere during the exigencies of the war, and we so certified upon the face of the claims. A similar principle guided our decision upon several claims for the rent of vacant lots in Cairo, which had been used by the military authorities for the erection of temporary barracks or stables. We determined that for these no rent ought, under the circumstances, to be allowed, but we suggested that in justice to the owners this temporary occupation should be terminated as soon as possible by the sale and removal of the buildings.

A very small percentage of the claims were rejected because of fraud. In almost every case it was possible to suppose that the apparent fraud was accident. My observation throughout the war was the same. I do not believe that so much business could be transacted with a closer adherence to the line of honesty. That there were frauds is a matter of course, because men, and even some women, are wicked, but frauds were the exception.

Our commission finished its labors at Cairo on July 31, 1862, and I went at once to Washington with the report, placing it in the hands of Mr. Stanton on August 5th. It was never printed, and the manuscript is still in the files of the War Department.

There was a great deal of curiosity among officers in Washington about the result of our investigation, and all the time that I was in the city I was being questioned on the subject. It was natural enough that they should have felt interested in our report. The charges of fraud and corruption against officers and contractors had become so reckless and general that the mere sight of a man in conference with a high official led to the suspicion and often the charge that he was conspiring to rob the Government. That in this case, where the charges seemed so well based, so small a percentage of corruption had been proved was a source of solid satisfaction to everyone in the War Department.

All the leisure that I had while in Cairo I spent in horseback riding up and down the river banks and in visiting the adjacent military posts. My longest and most interesting trip was on the Fourth of July, when I went down the Mississippi to attend a big celebration at Memphis. I remember it particularly because it was there that I first met General Grant. The officers stationed in the city gave a dinner that day, to which I was invited. At the table I was seated between Grant and Major John A. Rawlins, of his staff. I remember distinctly the pleasant impression Grant made—that of a man of simple manners, straightforward, cordial, and unpretending. He had already fought the successful battles of Fort Donelson and Shiloh, and, when I met him, was a major general in command of the district of West Tennessee, Department of the Missouri, under [General Henry] Halleck, with headquarters at Memphis. Although one would not have suspected it from his manners, he was really under a cloud at the time because of his operations at Shiloh. Those who did not like Grant had accused him of having been taken by surprise there, and had declared that he would have been beaten if [General Don Carlos] Buell had not come up. I often talked later with Grant's staff officers about Shiloh, and they always affirmed that he would have been successful if Buell had not come to his relief. I believe Grant himself thought so, although he never said so directly in any one of the many talks I had with him about the battle.

AT THE FRONT WITH GRANT'S ARMY

As Mr. Stanton had no immediate need of my services, I returned in August to New York, where I was occupied with various private affairs until the middle of November, when I received a telegram from Assistant Secretary-of-War P. H. Watson, asking me to go immediately to Washington to enter upon another investigation. I went, and was received by Mr. Stanton, who offered me the place of Assistant Secretary of War. I said I would accept.

"All right," said he; "consider it settled."

As I went out from the War Department into the street I met Major Charles G. Halpine—"Miles O'Reilly"—of the Sixty-ninth New York Infantry. I had known Halpine well as a newspaper man in New York, and I told him of my appointment as Mr. Stanton's assistant. He immediately repeated what I had told him to some newspaper people. It was reported in the New York papers the next morning. The Secretary was greatly offended and withdrew the appointment. When I told Halpine I had, of course, no idea he was going to repeat it; besides, I did not think there was any harm in telling.

Immediately after this episode I formed a partnership with Roscoe Conkling and George W. Chadwick to buy cotton.

Conkling (1829 – 1888), politician and influential New York political-machine leader. He was critical to getting Chester Arthur on the ticket as James Garfield's Vice President.—Ed. 2018

The outcry which the manufacturers had raised over the inability to get cotton for their industries had induced the Government to permit trading through the lines of the army, and the business looked profitable. Conkling and I each put ten thousand dollars into the firm, and Chadwick gave his services, which, as he was an expert in cotton, was considered equal to our capital. To facilitate our operations, I went to Washington to ask Mr. Stanton for letters of recommendation to the generals on and near the Mississippi, where we proposed to begin our purchases.

Mr. Stanton and I had several conversations about the advisability of allowing such traffic, but he did not hesitate about giving me the letters I asked. There were several of them: one to General Hurlbut, then at Memphis; another to General Grant, who had begun his movement against Vicksburg; and another to General Curtis, who commanded in Arkansas. The general purport of them was: "Mr. Dana is my friend; you can rely upon what he says, and if you can be kind to him in any way you will oblige me."

It was in January, 1863, that Chadwick and I went to Memphis, where we stayed at the Gayoso House, at that time the swell hotel of the town and the headquarters of several officers.

It was not long after I began to study the trade in cotton before I saw it was a bad business and ought to be stopped. I at once wrote Mr. Stanton the following letter, which embodied my observations and gave my opinion as to what should be done:

Memphis, January 21, 1863.

Dear Sir: You will remember our conversations on the subject of excluding cotton speculators from the regions occupied by our armies in the South. I now write to urge the matter upon your attention as a measure of military necessity.

The mania for sudden fortunes made in cotton, raging in a vast population of Jews and Yankees scattered throughout this whole country, and in this town almost exceeding the numbers of the regular residents, has to an alarming extent corrupted and demoralized the army. Every colonel, captain, or quartermaster is in secret partnership with some operator in cotton; every soldier dreams of adding a bale of cotton to his monthly pay. I had no conception of the extent of this evil until I came and saw for myself.

Besides, the resources of the rebels are inordinately increased from this source. Plenty of cotton is brought in from beyond our lines, especially by the agency of Jewish traders, who pay for it ostensibly in Treasury notes, but really in gold.

What I would propose is that no private purchaser of cotton shall be allowed in any part of the occupied region.

Let quartermasters buy the article at a fixed price, say twenty or twenty-five cents per pound, and forward it by army transportation to proper centers, say Helena, Memphis, or Cincinnati, to be sold at public auction on Government account. Let the sales take place on regular fixed days, so that all parties desirous of buying can be sure when to be present.

But little capital will be required for such an operation. The sales being frequent and for cash, will constantly replace the amount employed for the purpose. I should say that two hundred thousand dollars would be sufficient to conduct the movement.

I have no doubt that this two hundred thousand dollars so employed would be more than equal to thirty thousand men added to the national armies.

My pecuniary interest is in the continuance of the present state of things, for while it lasts there are occasional opportunities of profit to be made by a daring operator; but I should be false to my duty did I, on that account, fail to implore you to put an end to an evil so-enormous, so insidious, and so full of peril to the country.

My first impulse was to hurry to Washington to represent these things to you in person; but my engagements here with other persons will not allow me to return East so speedily. I beg you, however, to act without delay, if possible. An excellent man to put at the head of the business would be General Strong. I make this suggestion without any idea whether the employment would be agreeable to him.

Yours faithfully,

Charles A. Dana.

P. S.—Since writing the above I have seen General Grant, who fully agrees with all my statements and suggestions, except that imputing corruption to every officer, which of course I did not intend to be taken literally.

I have also just attended a public sale by the quartermaster here of five hundred bales of cotton confiscated by General Grant at Oxford and Holly Springs. It belonged to Jacob Thompson and other notorious rebels. This cotton brought today over a million and a half of dollars, cash. This sum alone would be five times enough to set on foot the system I recommend, without drawing upon the

Treasury at all. In fact, there can be no question that by adopting this system the quartermaster's department in this valley would become self-supporting, while the army would become honest again, and the slaveholders would no longer find that the rebellion had quadrupled the price of their great staple, but only doubled it.

See also, Among the Cotton Thieves.—Ed. 2018

As soon as I could get away from Memphis I went to Washington, where I had many conversations with Mr. Lincoln and Mr. Stanton about restricting the trade in cotton. They were deeply interested in my observations, and questioned me closely about what I had seen. My opinion that the trade should be stopped had the more weight because I was able to say, "General Grant and every general officer whom I have seen hopes it will be done."

The result of these consultations was that on March 31, 1863, Mr. Lincoln issued a proclamation declaring unlawful all commercial intercourse with the States in insurrection, except when carried on according to the regulations prescribed by the Secretary of the Treasury. These regulations Mr. Chase prepared at once. At the same time that Mr. Lincoln issued his proclamation, Mr. Stanton issued an order forbidding officers and all members of the army to have anything to do with the trade. In spite of all these regulations, however, and the modifications of them which experience brought, there was throughout the war more or less difficulty over cotton trading.

From Washington I went back to New York. I had not been there long before Mr. Stanton sent for me to come to Washington. He wanted someone to go to Grant's army, he said, to report daily to him the military proceedings, and to give such information as would enable Mr. Lincoln and himself to settle their minds as to Grant, about whom at that time there were many doubts, and against whom there was some complaint.

"Will you go?" Mr. Stanton asked. "Yes," I said. "Very well," he replied. "The ostensible function I shall give you will be that of special commissioner of the War Department to investigate the pay service of the Western armies, but your real duty will be to report to me every day what you see."

On March 12th Mr. Stanton wrote me the following letter:

War Department, Washington City,

March 12, 1863.

Dear Sir: I inclose you a copy of your order of appointment and the order fixing your compensation, with a letter to Generals Sumner,* Grant, and Rosecrans, and a draft for one thousand dollars. Having explained the purposes of your appointment to you personally, no further instructions will be given unless specially required. Please acknowledge the receipt of this, and proceed as early as possible to your duties.

Yours truly,

Edwin M. Stanton.

My commission read:

Ordered, That C. A. Dana, Esq., be and he is hereby appointed special commissioner of the War Department to investigate and report upon the condition of the pay service in the Western armies. All paymasters and assistant paymasters will furnish to the said commissioner for the Secretary of War information upon any matters concerning which he may make inquiry of them as fully and completely and promptly as if directly called for by the Secretary of War. Railroad agents, quartermasters, and commissioners will give him transportation and subsistence. All officers and persons in the service will aid him in the performance of his duties, and will afford him assistance, courtesy, and protection. The said commissioner will make report to this department as occasion may require.

The letters of introduction and explanation to the generals were identical:

General: Charles A. Dana, Esq., has been appointed a special commissioner of this department to investigate and report upon the condition of the pay service in the Western armies. You will please aid him in the performance of his duties, and communicate to him fully your views and wishes in respect to that branch of the service in your command, and also give to him such information as you may deem beneficial to the service. He is specially commended to your courtesy and protection. Yours truly,

Edwin M. Stanton.

I started at once for Memphis, going by way of Cairo and Columbus.

I sent my first dispatch to the War Department from Columbus, on March 20th. It was sent by a secret cipher furnished by the War Department, which I used myself, for throughout the war I was my own cipher clerk. The ordinary method at the various headquarters was for the sender to write out the dispatch in full, after which it was translated from plain English into the agreed cipher by a telegraph operator or clerk retained for that exclusive purpose, who understood it, and by another it was retranslated back again at the other end of the line. So whatever military secret was transmitted was at the mercy always of at least two outside persons, besides running the gantlet of other prying eyes. Dispatches written in complex cipher codes were often difficult to unravel, unless transmitted by the operator with the greatest precision. A wrong word sometimes destroyed the sense of an entire dispatch, and important movements were delayed thereby. This explains the oft-repeated "I do not understand your telegram" found in the official correspondence of the war period.

I have become familiar since the war with a great many ciphers, but I never found one which was more satisfactory than that which I used in my messages to Mr. Stanton. In preparing my message I first wrote it out in lines of a given number of words, spaced regularly so as to form five, six, seven, eight, nine, and ten columns. My key contained various "routes," to be followed in writing out the messages for transmission. Thus, a five-column message had one route, a six-column another, and so on. The route was indicated by a "commencement word." If I had put my message into five columns, I would write at the beginning the word "Army," or any one in a list of nine words. The receiver, on looking for that word in his key, would see that he was to write out what he had received in lines of five words, thus forming five columns; and then he was to read it down the fifth column, up the third, down the fourth, up the second, down the first. At the end of each column an "extra" or "check" word was added as a blind. A list of "blind" words was also printed in the key, with each route, which could be inserted, if wished, at the end of each line so as still further to deceive curious people who did not have the key. The key contained also a large number of cipher words. Thus, P. H. Sheridan was "soap" or "Somerset"; President was "Pembroke" or "Penfield." Instead of writing "there has been," I wrote "maroon"; instead of secession, "mint"; instead of Vicksburg, "Cupid." My own cipher was "spunky" or "squad." The days, months, hours, numerals, and alphabet all had ciphers.

The only message sent by this cipher to be translated by an outsider on the route, so far as I know, was that one of 4 p. m., September 20, 1863, in which I reported the Union defeat at Chickamauga. General R. S. Granger, who was then at Nashville, was at the telegraph office waiting for news when my dispatch passed through. The operator guessed out the dispatch, as he afterward confessed, and it was passed around Nashville. The agent of the Associated Press at Louisville sent out a private printed circular quoting me as an authority for reporting the battle as a total defeat, and in Cincinnati Horace Maynard repeated, the same day of the battle, the entire second sentence of the dispatch,

"Chickamauga is as fatal a name in our history as Bull Run."

This premature disclosure to the public of what was only the truth, well known at the front, caused a great deal of trouble. I immediately set on foot an investigation to discover who had penetrated our cipher code, and soon arrived at a satisfactory understanding of the matter, of which Mr. Stanton was duly informed. No blame could attach to me, as was manifest upon the inquiry; nevertheless, the sensation resulted in considerable annoyance all along the line from Chattanooga to Washington. I suggested to Mr. Stanton the advisability of concocting a new and more difficult cipher, but it was never changed, so far as I now remember.

It was from Columbus, Ky., on March 20, 1863, that I sent my first telegram to the War Department. I did not remain in Columbus long, for there was absolutely no trustworthy information there respecting affairs down the river, but took a boat to Memphis, where I arrived on March 23d. I found General [Stephen] Hurlbut in command. I had met Hurlbut in January, when on my cotton business, and he gave me every opportunity to gather information concerning the operations against Vicksburg. Four different plans for reaching the city were then on foot, the essential element of all of them being to secure for the army on the high ground behind the city a foothold whence it could strike, and at the same time be supplied from a river base. The first and oldest and apparently most promising of these plans was that of the canal across the neck of the peninsula facing Vicksburg, on the Louisiana side. When I reached Memphis this canal was thought to be nearly done.

The second route was by Lake Providence, about forty miles north of Vicksburg, in Louisiana. It was close to the western bank of the Mississippi, with which it was proposed to connect it by means of a canal. The Bayou Macon connected Lake Providence with the Tensas River. By descending the Tensas to the Washita, the Washita to the Red, the Red to the Mississippi, the army could be landed on the east bank of the Mississippi about one hundred and fifty miles south of Vicksburg, and thence could be marched north. McPherson, with his Seventeenth Corps, had been ordered by Grant on January 30th to open this route. It was reported at Memphis when I arrived there that the cutting of Lake Providence was perfectly successful, but that Bayou Macon was full of snags, which must be got out before the Tensas would be accessible.

The third and fourth routes proposed for getting behind Vicksburg—namely, by Yazoo Pass and Steele's Bayou—were attracting the chief attention when I reached Memphis. Yazoo Pass opened from the eastern bank of the Mississippi at a point about one hundred and fifty miles above Vicksburg into Moon Lake, and thence into the Coldwater River. Through the Cold water and the Tallahatchie the Yazoo River was reached. If troops could follow this route and capture Haynes's Bluff, fourteen miles from the mouth of the Yazoo, Vicksburg at once became untenable. The Yazoo Pass operation had begun in February, but the detachment had had bad luck, and on my arrival at Memphis was lying up the Yallabusha waiting for reinforcements and supplies.

An attempt was being made also to reach the Yazoo by a roundabout route through Steele's Bayou, Deer Creek, the Rolling Fork, and the Big Sunflower. Grant had learned of this route only a short time before my arrival, and had at once sent Sherman with troops and Admiral Porter with gunboats to attempt to reach the Yazoo. On March 27th reports came to Memphis that Sherman had landed twenty regiments on the east bank of the Yazoo above Haynes's Bluff, and that the gunboats were there to support him. Reports from other points also were so encouraging that the greatest enthusiasm prevailed throughout the army, and General Grant was said to be dead sure he would have Vicksburg within a fortnight.

Five days later, however, we heard at Memphis that there had been a series of disasters in these different operations, that the Yazoo Pass expedition was definitely abandoned, and that General Grant had an entirely new plan of campaign.

I had not been long at Memphis before I decided that it was impossible to gather trustworthy news there. I had to rely for most of my information on the reports brought up the river by occasional officers, not all of whom were sure of what they told, and on the stories of persons coming from the vicinity of the different operations. Occasionally an intelligent planter arrived whom I was inclined to believe, but on the whole I found that my sources of information were few and uncertain. I accordingly suggested to Mr. Stanton, three days after my arrival, that I would be more useful farther down the river. In reply he telegraphed:

War Department, Washington City,

March 30, 1863.

C. A. Dana, Esq., Memphis, Tenn., via Cairo :

Your telegrams have been received, and although the information has been meager and unsatisfactory, I am conscious that arises from no fault of yours. You will proceed to General Grant's headquarters, or wherever you may be best able to accomplish the purposes designated by this department. You will consider your movements to be governed by your own discretion, without any restriction.

Edwin M. Stanton,

Secretary of War.

As soon after receiving his telegram as I could get a boat I left Memphis for Milliken's Bend, where General Grant had his headquarters. I reached there at noon on April 6th.

The Mississippi at Milliken's Bend was a mile wide, and the sight as we came down the river by boat was most imposing. Grant's big army was stretched up and down the river bank over the plantations, its white tents affording a new decoration to the natural magnificence of the broad plains. These plains, which stretch far back from the river, were divided into rich and old plantations by blooming hedges of rose and Osage orange, the mansions of the owners being inclosed in roses, myrtles, magnolias, oaks, and every other sort of beautiful and noble trees. The negroes whose work made all this wealth and magnificence were gone, and there was nothing growing in the fields.

For some days after my arrival I lived in a steamboat tied up to the shore, for though my tent was pitched and ready, I was not able to get a mattress and pillow. From the deck of the steamer I saw in those days many a wonderful and to me novel sight. One I remember still. I was standing out on the upper deck with a group of officers, when we saw far away, dose to the other shore of the river, a long line of something white floating in the water. We thought it was foam, but it was too long and white, and that it was cotton which had been thrown into the river, but it was too straight and regular. Presently we heard a gun fired, then another, and then we saw it was an enormous flock of swans. They arose from the water one after the other, and sailed away up the river in long, curving, silver lines, bending and floating almost like clouds, and finally disappearing high up in the air above the green woods on the Mississippi shore. I suppose there were a thousand of them.

I had not been long at Milliken's Bend before I was on friendly terms with all the generals, big and little, and one or two of them I found were very rare men. Sherman especially impressed me as a man of genius and of the widest intellectual acquisitions. Every day I rode in one direction or another with an officer, inspecting the operations going on. From what I saw on my rides over the country I got a new insight into slavery, which made me no more a friend to that institution than I was before. I had seen slavery in Maryland, Kentucky, Virginia, and Missouri, but it was not till I saw these great Louisiana plantations with all their apparatus for living and working that I really felt the aristocratic nature of the institution, and the infernal baseness of that aristocracy. Every day my conviction was intensified that the territorial and political integrity of the nation must be preserved at all costs, no matter how long it took; that it was better to keep up the existing war as long as was necessary, rather than to make arrangement for indefinite wars hereafter and for other disruptions; that we must have it out then, and settle forever the question, so that our children would be able to attend to other matters. For my own part, I preferred one nation and one country, with a military government afterward, if such should follow,' rather than two or three nations and countries with the semblance of the old Constitution in each of them, ending in wars and despotisms everywhere.

As soon as I arrived at Milliken's Bend, on April 6th, I had hunted up Grant and explained my mission.

He received me cordially. Indeed, I think Grant was always glad to have me with his army. He did not like letter writing, and my daily dispatches to Mr. Stanton relieved him from the necessity of describing every day what was going on in the army. From the first neither he nor any of his staff or corps commanders evinced any unwillingness to show me the inside of things. In this first interview at Milliken's Bend, for instance, Grant explained to me so fully his new plan of campaign—for there was now but one—that by three o'clock I was able to send an outline of it to Mr. Stanton. From that time I saw and knew all the interior operations of that toughest of tough jobs, the reopening of the Mississippi.

The new project, so Grant told me, was to transfer his army to New Carthage, and from there carry it over the Mississippi, landing it at or about Grand Gulf; to capture this point, and then to operate rapidly on the southern and eastern shore of the Big Black River, threatening at the same time both Vicksburg and Jackson, and confusing the Confederates as to his real objective. If this could be done he believed the enemy; would come out of Vicksburg and fight.

The first element in this plan was to open a passage from the Mississippi near Milliken's Bend, above Vicksburg, to the bayou on the west side, which led around to New Carthage below. The length of navigation in this cut-off was about thirty-seven miles, and the plan was to take through with small tugs perhaps fifty barges, enough, at least, to transfer the whole army, with artillery and baggage, to the other side of the Mississippi in twenty-four hours. If necessary, troops were to be transported by the canal, though Grant hoped to march them by the road along its bank. Part of McClernand's corps had already reached New Carthage overland, and Grant was hurrying other troops forward. The canal to the bayou was already half completed, thirty-five hundred men being at work on it when I arrived.

The second part of the plan was to float down the river, past the Vicksburg batteries, half a dozen steamboats protected by defenses of bales of cotton and wet hay; these steamboats were to serve as transports of supplies after the army had crossed the Mississippi.

Perhaps the best evidence of the feasibility of the project was found in the fact that the river men pronounced its success certain. General Sherman, who commanded one of the three corps in Grant's army, and with whom I conversed at length upon the subject, thought there was no difficulty in opening the passage, but that the line would be a precarious one for supplies after the army was thrown across the Mississippi. Sher- man's preference was for a movement by way of Yazoo Pass, or Lake Providence, but it was not long before I saw in our daily talks that his mind was tending to the conclusion of General Grant. As for General Grant, his purpose was dead set on the new scheme. Admiral Porter cordially agreed with him.

An important modification was made a few days after my arrival in the plan of operations. It was determined that after the occupation of Grand Gulf the main army, instead of operating up the Big Black toward Jackson, should proceed down the river against Port Hudson, co-operating with General Banks against that point, and that after the capture of Port Hudson the two united forces should proceed against Vicksburg.

There seemed to be only one hitch in the campaign. Grant had entrusted the attack on Grand Gulf to [General John] McClernand [Illinois politician and a friend of Lincoln]. Sherman, [Admiral David Dixon] Porter, and other leading officers believed this a mistake, and talked frankly with me about it. One night when we had all gathered at Grant's headquarters and were talking over the campaign very freely, as we were accustomed to do, both Sherman and Porter protested against the arrangement. But Grant would not be changed. McClernand, he said, was exceedingly desirous of the command. He was the senior of the other corps commanders. He was an especial favorite of the President, and the position which his corps occupied on the ground when the movement was first projected was such that the advance naturally fell to its lot; besides, he had entered zealously into the plan from the first, while Sherman had doubted and criticized, and [James] McPherson, whom Grant said he would really have much preferred, was away at Lake Providence, and though he had approved of the scheme, he had taken no active part in it.

I believed the assignment of this duty to McClernand to be so dangerous that I added my expostulation to those of the generals, and in reporting the case to Mr. Stanton I wrote: "I have remonstrated so far as I could properly do so against entrusting so momentous an operation to McClernand."

Mr. Stanton replied: "Allow me to suggest that you carefully avoid giving any advice in respect to commands that may be assigned, as it may lead to misunderstanding and troublesome complications." Of course, after that I scrupulously observed his directions, even in extreme cases.

As the days went on everybody, in spite of this hitch, became more sanguine that the new project would succeed. For my part I had not a doubt of it, as one can see from this fragment written from Milliken's Bend on April 13th to one of my friends:

> "Like all who really know the facts, I feel no sort of doubt that we shall before long get the nut cracked. Probably before this letter reaches New York on its way to you the telegraph will get ahead of it with the news that Grant, masking Vicksburg, deemed impregnable by its defenders, has carried the bulk of his army down the river through a cut-off which he has opened without the enemy believing it could be done; has occupied Grand Gulf, taken Port Hudson, and, effecting a junction with the forces of Banks, has returned up the river to threaten Jackson and compel the enemy to come out of Vicksburg and fight him on ground of his own choosing. Of course this scheme may miscarry in whole or in parts, but as yet the chances all favor its execution, which is now just ready to begin."

BEFORE AND AROUND VICKSBURG

On the new lines adopted by General Grant, the work went on cheeringly, though every day changes were made in the details. I spent my days in riding from point to point, noting the progress. I went out often with Colonel G. G. Pride, the engineer officer, in whose mess I was, and who was superintending the construction of the canal which led from Duckport to the bayou. The work on this canal was a curious sight to see, for there was a force equal to five regiments at the digging, while a large number of pioneers were engaged in clearing the bayou beyond. The canal was opened on April 13th, and the authorities agreed that there was no reason to doubt its usefulness, though the obstructions in the bayou were so numerous that it was thought that it would require several days more to clear a passage for tugs and barges.

One of my most interesting trips from Milliken's Bend was made with Major James H. Wilson to view the casemated batteries our engineers were constructing on the shore opposite Vicksburg.

James Harrison Wilson (1837 – 1925) was an extremely effective officer and a favorite of Rawlins and Dana. He played vital roles in the western and eastern theaters during the war. After the war, he was a prolific author. See is excellent memoir, Under the Old Flag. *—Ed. 2018*

They hoped with the thirty-pound Parrotts they were putting in to be able to destroy any building in the town. From behind the levee of the peninsula we were able with our glasses to examine the fortifications of Vicksburg.

The best look I had at that town, however, while I was at Milliken's Bend was not from the peninsula opposite, but from a gunboat. On April 12th I went down with a flag of truce to the vicinity of Vicksburg, so that I got a capital view. It was an ugly place, with its line of bluffs commanding the channel for fully seven miles, and battery piled above battery all the way.

Admiral Porter's arrangements for carrying out the second part of Grant's scheme—that is, running the Vicksburg batteries—were all completed by April 16th, the ironclads and steamers being protected in vulnerable parts by bulwarks of hay, cotton, and sand bags, and the barges loaded with forage, coal, and the camp equipment of General McClernand's corps, which was already at New Carthage. No doubt was felt that the design was known in Vicksburg, and it was arranged that Admiral Porter should open fire there with all his guns as he swept past the town, and that the new batteries on the levee opposite the city should also participate. Admiral Porter was to go with the expedition on a small tug, and he invited me to accompany him, but it seemed to me that I ought not to get out of my communications, and so refused. Instead, I joined Grant on his headquarters boat, which was stationed on the right bank of the river, where from the bows we could see the squadron as it started, and could follow its course until it was nearly past Vicksburg.

Just before ten o'clock on the night of April 16th the squadron cast loose its moorings. It was a strange scene. First a mass of black things detached itself from the shore, and we saw it float out toward the middle of the stream. There was nothing to be seen except this big black mass, which dropped slowly down the river. Soon another black mass detached itself, and another, then another. It was Admiral Porter's fleet of ironclad turtles, steamboats, and barges. They floated down the Mississippi darkly and silently, showing neither steam nor light, save occasionally a signal astern, where the enemy could not see it.

The vessels moved at intervals of about two hundred yards. First came seven ironclad turtles and one heavy armed ram ; following these were two side-wheel steamers and one stern-wheel, having twelve barges in tow; these barges carried the supplies. Far astern of them was one carrying ammunition. The most of the gunboats had already doubled the tongue of land which stretches northeasterly in front of Vicksburg, and they were immediately under the guns of nearly all the Confederate batteries, when there was a flash from the upper forts, and then for an hour and a half the cannonade was terrific, raging incessantly along the line of about four miles in extent. I counted five hundred and twenty-five discharges. Early in the action the enemy put the torch to a frame building in front of Vicksburg to light up the scene and direct his fire.

About 12.45 a. m. one our steamers, the *Henry Clay*, took fire, and burned for three quarters of an hour. The Henry Clay was lost by being abandoned by her captain and crew in a panic, they thinking her to be sinking. The pilot refused to go with them, and said if they would stay they would get her through safe. After they had fled in the yawls, the cotton bales on her deck took fire, and one wheel became unmanageable. The pilot then ran her aground, and got upon a plank, on which he was picked up four miles below.

The morning after Admiral Porter had run the Vicksburg batteries I went with General Grant to New Carthage to review the situation. We found the squadron there, all in fighting condition, though most of them had been hit. Not a man had been lost.

As soon as we returned to Milliken's Bend Grant ordered that six transport steamers, each loaded with one hundred thousand rations and forty days' coal, should be made ready to run the Vicksburg batteries. The order was executed on the night of the 22d. The transports were manned throughout, officers, engineers, pilots, and deck hands, by volunteers from the army, mainly from Logan's division. This dangerous service was sought with great eagerness, and experienced men had been found for every post. If ten thousand men had been wanted instead of one hundred and fifty, they would have engaged with zeal in the adventure. In addition to bulwarks of hay, cotton, and pork barrels, each transport was protected by a barge on each side of it. Orders were to drop noiselessly down with the current from the mouth of the Yazoo, and not show steam till the enemy's batteries began firing, when the boats were to use all their legs. The night was cloudy, and the run was made with the loss of one of the transports, the Tigress, which was sunk, and a few men wounded.

The day after these transports with supplies ran the Vicksburg batteries General Grant changed his headquarters to Smith's plantation, near New Carthage. All of McClernand's corps, the Thirteenth, was now near there, and that officer said ten thousand men would be ready to move from New Carthage the next day. McPherson's corps, which had been busy upon the Lake Providence expedition and other services, but which had been ordered to join, was now, except one division, moving over from Milliken's Bend. Sherman's corps, the Fifteenth, which had been stationed at Young's Point, was also under marching orders to New Carthage.

Grant's first object now was to cross the Mississippi as speedily as possible and capture Grand Gulf before it could be re-enforced; but first it was necessary to know the strength of this point. On the 22d Admiral Porter had gone down with his gunboats and opened fire to ascertain the position and strength of the batteries. He reported them too strong to overcome, and earnestly advised against a direct attack. He suggested that the troops either be marched down the west side from New Carthage to a point where they could be ferried over the Mississippi just below Grand Gulf, or that they be embarked on the transports and barges and floated past the batteries in the night.

The day after Grant changed his headquarters to Smith's plantation he went himself with General Porter to reconnoiter Grand Gulf. His reconnaissance convinced him that the place was not so strong as Admiral Porter had supposed, and an attack was ordered to be made as soon as the troops could be made ready, the next day, April 26th, if possible.

An irritating delay occurred then, however. McClernand's corps was not ready to move. When we came to Smith's plantation, on the 24th, I had seen that there was apparently much confusion in McClernand's command, and I was astonished to find, now that he was ordered to move across the Mississippi, that he was planning to carry his bride with her servants, and baggage along with him, although Grant had ordered that officers should leave behind everything that could impede the march.

On the 26th, the day when it was hoped to make an attack on Grand Gulf, I went with Grant by water from our headquarters at

Smith's plantation down to New Carthage and to Perkins's plantation below, where two of McClernand's divisions were encamped. These troops, it was supposed, were ready for immediate embarkation, and there were quite as many as all the transports could carry, but the first thing which struck us both on approaching the points of embarkation was that the steamboats and barges were scattered about in the river and in the bayou as if there was no idea of the imperative necessity of the promptest movement possible.

We at once steamed to Admiral Porter's flagship, which was lying just above Grand Gulf, and Grant sent for McClernand, ordering him to embark his men without losing a moment. In spite of this order, that night at dark, when a thunderstorm set in, not a single cannon or man had been moved. Instead, McClernand held a review of a brigade of Illinois troops at Perkins's about four o'clock in the afternoon. At the same time a salute of artillery was fired, notwithstanding the positive orders that had repeatedly been given to use no ammunition for any purpose except against the enemy.

When we got back from the river to headquarters, on the night of the 26th, we found that McPherson had arrived at Smith's plantation with the first division of his corps, the rear being not very far behind. His whole force would have been up the next day, but it was necessary to arrest its movements until McClernand could be got out of the way; this made McClernand's delay the more annoying. General Lorenzo Thomas, who was on the Mississippi at this time organizing negro troops, told me that he believed now that McPherson would actually have his men ready to embark before McClernand.

Early the next morning, April 27th, I went with Grant from Smith's plantation back to New Carthage. As soon as we arrived the general wrote a very severe letter to McClernand, but learning that at last the transport steamers and barges had been concentrated for use he did not send the rebuke. Grant spent the day there completing the preparations for embarking, and on the morning of the 28th about ten thousand men were on board. This force was not deemed sufficient for the attack on Grand Gulf, so the troops were brought down to Hard Times landing, on the Louisiana side, almost directly across the river from Grand Gulf, where a portion of them were debarked, and the transports sent back for Hovey's division, six thousand strong. We spent the night at Hard Times waiting for these troops, which arrived about daylight on the morning of the 29th.

There were now sixteen thousand men at Hard Times ready to be landed at the foot of the Grand Gulf bluff as soon as its batteries were silenced. At precisely eight o'clock the gunboats opened their attack. Seven, all ironclads, were engaged, and a cannonade was kept up for nearly six hours. We soon found that the enemy had five batteries, the first and most formidable of them being placed on the high promontory close to the mouth of the Big Black. The lower batteries, mounting smaller guns and having no more than two pieces each, were silenced early in the action, but this one obstinately resisted. For the last four hours of the engagement the whole seven gunboats were employed in firing at this one battery, now at long range, seeking to drop shells within the parapet, now at the very foot of the hill, within about two hundred yards, endeavoring to dismount its guns by direct fire. It was hit again and again, but its pieces were not disabled. At last, about half past one o'clock, Admiral Porter gave the signal to withdraw. The gunboats had been hit more or less severely. I was on board the *Benton* during the attack, and saw that her armor had been pierced repeatedly both in her sides and her pilot house, but she had not a gun disabled; and except for the holes through her mail, some of them in her hull, she was as ready to fight as at the beginning of the action.

The batteries having proved too much for the gunboats, General Grant determined to execute an alternative plan which he had had in mind from the first; that was, to debark the troops and march them south across the peninsula which faces Grand Gulf to a place out of reach of the Confederate guns. While the engagement between the gunboats and batteries had been going on, all the rest of McClernand's corps had reached Hard Times, having marched around by land, and three divisions of McPherson's corps had also come up. This entire body of about thirty-five thousand men was immediately started across the peninsula to De Shroon's plantation, where it was proposed to embark them again.

Late in the evening I left Hard Times with Grant to ride across the peninsula to De Shroon's. The night was pitch dark, and, as we rode side by side, Grant's horse suddenly gave a nasty stumble. I expected to see the general go over the animal's head, and I watched intently, not to see if he was hurt, but if he would show any anger. I had been with Grant daily now for three weeks, and I had never seen him ruffled or heard him swear. His equanimity was becoming a curious spectacle to me. When I saw his horse lunge my first thought was, "Now he will swear." For an instant his moral status was on trial; but Grant was a tenacious horseman, and instead of going over the animal's head, as I imagined he would, he kept his seat. Pulling up his horse, he rode on, and, to my utter amazement, without a word or sign of impatience. And it is a fact that though I was with Grant during the most trying campaigns of the war, I never heard him use an oath.

Grant was a superb equestrian and famously imperturbable. He never swore. When asked about it by his aide, Horace Porter, he merely said, "I never developed the habit."—Ed. 2018

In order to get the transports past Grand Gulf, Porter's gunboats had engaged the batteries about dusk. This artillery duel lasted until about ten o'clock, the gunboats withdrawing as soon as the transports were safely past, and steaming at once to De Shroon's plantation, where General McClernand's corps was all ready to take the transports. The night was spent in embarking the men. By eleven o'clock the next morning, April 30th, three divisions were landed on the east shore of the Mississippi at the place General Grant had selected. This was Bruinsburg, sixty miles south of Vicksburg, and the first point south of Grand Gulf from which the highlands of the interior could be reached by a road over dry land.

I was obliged to separate from Grant on the 30th, for the means for transporting troops and officers were so limited that neither an extra man nor a particle of unnecessary baggage was allowed, and I did not get over until the morning of May 1st, after the army had moved on Port Gibson, where they first engaged the enemy. As soon as I was landed at Bruinsburg I started in the direction of the battle, on foot, of course, as no horses had been brought over. I had not gone far before I overtook a quartermaster driving toward Port Gibson; he took me into his wagon. About four miles from Port Gibson we came upon the first signs of the battle, a field where it was evident that there had been a struggle. I got out of the wagon as we approached, and started toward a little white house with green blinds, covered with vines. The little white house had been taken as a field hospital, and the first thing my eyes fell upon as I went into the yard was a heap of arms and legs which had been amputated and thrown into a pile outside. I had seen men shot and dead men plenty, but this pile of legs and arms gave me a vivid sense of war such as I had not before experienced.

As the army was pressing the Confederates toward Port Gibson all that day I followed in the rear, without overtaking General Grant. While trailing along after the Union forces I came across Fred Grant, then a lad of thirteen, who had been left asleep by his father on a steamer at Bruinsburg, but who had started out on foot like myself as soon as he awoke and found the army had marched. We tramped and foraged together until the next morning, when some officers who had captured two old horses gave us each one. We got the best bridles and saddles we could, and thus equipped made our way into Port Gibson, which the enemy had deserted and where General Grant now had his headquarters. I rode that old horse for four or five days, then by a chance I got a good one. A captured Confederate officer had been brought before General Grant for examination. Now this man had a very good horse, and after Grant had finished his questions the officer said:

"General, this horse and saddle are my private property; they do not belong to the Confederate army; they belong to me as a citizen, and I trust you will let me have them. Of course, while I am a prisoner I do not expect to be allowed to ride the horse, but I hope you will regard him as my property, and finally restore him to me."

"Well," said Grant, "I have got four or five first-rate horses wandering somewhere about the Southern Confederacy. They have been captured from me in battle or by spies. I will authorize you, whenever you find one of them, to take possession of him. I cheerfully give him to you; but as for this horse, I think he is just about the horse Mr. Dana needs."

I rode my new acquisition afterward through that whole campaign, and when I came away I turned him over to the quartermaster. Whenever I went out with General Grant anywhere he always had some question to ask about that horse.

IN CAMP AND BATTLE WITH GRANT AND HIS GENERALS

It was the second day of May, 1863, when I rode into Port Gibson, Miss., and inquired for Grant's headquarters. I found the general in a little house of the village, busily directing the advance of the army. He told me that in the battle of the day before the Confederates had been driven back on the roads to Grand Gulf and Vicksburg, and that our forces were now in full pursuit. By the next morning, May 3d, our troops had possession of the roads as far as the Big Black. As soon as he was sure of this, General Grant started with a brigade of infantry and some twenty cavalrymen for Grand Gulf. I accompanied him on the trip. When within about seven miles of Grand Gulf we found that the town had been deserted, and leaving the brigade we entered with the cavalry escort.

During this ride to Grand Gulf Grant made inquiries on every side about the food supplies of the country we were entering. He told me he had been gathering in- formation on this point ever since the army crossed the Mississippi, and had made up his mind that both beef and cattle and corn were abundant in the country. The result of this inquiry was that here at Grand Gulf Grant took the resolve which makes the Vicksburg campaign so famous—that of abandoning entirely his base of supplies as soon as the army was all up and the rations on the way arrived, boldly striking into the interior, and depending on the country for meat and even for bread.

We did not reach Grand Gulf until late on May 3d, but at one o'clock on the morning of the 4th Grant was off for the front. He had decided that it was useless to bring up the army to this place, to the capture of which we had been so long looking, and which had been abandoned so quickly now that our army was across the Mississippi. I did not follow until later in the day, and so had an opportunity of seeing General Sherman. His corps was marching from above as rapidly as possible down to Hard Times landing, and he had come over to Grand Gulf to see about debarking his troops there; this he succeeded in doing a couple of days later.

That evening I joined Grant at his new headquarters at Hankinson's Ferry on the Big Black, and now began my first experience with army marching into an enemy's territory. A glimpse of my life at this time is given in a letter to a child, written the morning after I rejoined Grant:

"All of a sudden it is very cold here. Two days ago it was hot like summer, but now I sit in my tent in my overcoat, writing, and thinking if I only were at home instead of being almost two thousand miles away.

"Away yonder, in the edge of the woods, I hear the drum-beat that calls the soldiers to their supper. It is only a little after five o'clock, but they begin the day very early and end it early. Pretty soon after dark they are all asleep, lying in their blankets under the trees, for in a quick march they leave their tents behind. Their guns are all ready at their sides, so that if they are suddenly called at night they can start in a moment. It is strange in the morning before daylight to hear the bugle and drums sound the reveille, which calls the army to wake up. It will begin perhaps at a distance and then run along the whole line, bugle after bugle and drum after drum taking it up, and then it goes from front to rear, farther and farther away, the sweet sounds throbbing and rolling while you lie on the grass with your saddle for a pillow, half awake, or opening your eyes to see that the stars are all bright in the sky, or that there is only a faint flush in the east, where the day is soon to break.

"Living in camp is queer business. I get my meals in General Grant's mess, and pay my share of the expenses. The table is a chest with a double cover, which unfolds on the right and the left; the dishes, knives and forks, and caster are inside. Sometimes we get good things, but generally we don't. The cook is an old negro, black and grimy. The cooking is not as clean as it might be, but in war you can't be particular about such things.

"The plums and peaches here are pretty nearly ripe. The strawberries have been ripe these few days, but the soldiers eat them up before we get a sight of them. The figs are as big as the end of your thumb, and the green pears are big enough to eat. But you don't know what beautiful flower gardens there are here. I never saw such roses; and the other day I found a lily as big as a tiger lily, only it was a magnificent red."

Grant's policy now was to push the Confederates ahead of him up the Big Black River, threatening Jackson, the State capital, and the Big Black bridge behind Vicksburg, and capturing both if necessary. His opinion was that this maneuver would draw Pemberton out of Vicksburg and bring on a decisive battle within ten days.

From Hankinson's Ferry, the headquarters were changed on the 7th to Rocky Springs, and there we remained until the 11th. By that time McClernand and McPherson had advanced to within ten or twelve miles of the railroad which runs from Vicksburg to Jackson, and were lying nearly in an east and west line; and Sherman's entire corps had reached Hankinson's Ferry. Supplies which Grant had ordered from Milliken's Bend had also arrived. The order was now given to Sherman to destroy the bridge at Hankinson's Ferry, the rear guards were abandoned, and our communications cut. So complete was our isolation that it was ten days after we left Rocky Springs, on May 11th, before I was able to get another dispatch to Mr. Stanton.

This march toward Jackson proved to be no easy affair. More than one night I bivouacked on the ground in the rain after being all day in my saddle. The most comfortable night I had, in fact, was in a church of which the officers had taken possession. Having no pillow, I went up to the pulpit and borrowed the Bible for the night. Dr. H. L. Hewitt, who was medical director on Grant's staff, slept near me, and he always charged me afterward with stealing that Bible.

In spite of the roughness of our life, it was all of intense interest to me, particularly the condition of the people over whose country we were marching. A fact which impressed me was the total absence of men capable of bearing arms. Only old men and children remained. The young men were all in the army or had perished in it. The South was drained of its youth. An army of half a million with a white population of only five millions to draw upon, must soon finish the stock of raw material for soldiers. Another fact of moment was that we found men who had at the first sympathized with the rebellion, and even joined in it, now of their own accord rendering Grant the most valuable assistance, in order that the rebellion might be ended as speedily as possible, and something saved by the Southern people out of the otherwise total and hopeless ruin. "Slavery is gone, other property is mainly gone," they said, "but, for God's sake, let us save some relic of our former means of living."

In this forward movement the left of the army was ordered to hug the Big Black as closely as possible, while the right moved straight on Raymond. On the 12th, the right wing, under McPherson, met the enemy just west of Raymond. Grant at the time had his headquarters about at the center of the army, with Sherman's corps, some seven miles west of Raymond. I left him to go to the scene of the battle at once. It was a hard-fought engagement, lasting some three hours. McPherson drove the Confederates back to and through Raymond, and there stopped. The next day the advance of the army toward Jackson was continued. It rained heavily on the march and the roads were very heavy, but the troops were in the best of spirits at their successes and prospects. This work was a great improvement on digging canals and running batteries. On the afternoon of the 14th, about two and a half miles west of Jackson, McPherson and Sherman were temporarily stopped by the enemy, but he was quickly defeated, and that night we entered the capital of Mississippi.

At Jackson I received an important telegram from Stanton, though how it got to me there I do not remember. General Grant had been much troubled by the delay McClernand had caused at New Carthage, but he had felt reluctant to remove him as he had been assigned to his command by the President. My reports to the Secretary on the situation had convinced him that Grant ought to have perfect independence in the matter, so he telegraphed me as follows:

Washington, D. C.,

May 6, 1863.

C. A. Dana, Esq., Smith's Plantation, Ia.

General Grant has full and absolute authority to enforce his own commands and to remove any person who by ignorance in action or any cause interferes with or delays his operations. He has the full confidence of the Government, is expected to enforce his authority, and will be firmly and heartily supported, but he will be responsible for any failure to exert his powers. You may communicate this to him.

E. M. Stanton,

Secretary of War.

The very evening of the day that we reached Jackson, Grant learned that Lieutenant-General Pemberton had been ordered by General Joe Johnston to come out of Vicksburg and attack our rear. Grant immediately faced the bulk of his army about to meet the enemy, leaving Sherman in Jackson to tear up the railroads and destroy all the public property there that could be of use to the Confederates. I remained with Sherman to see the work of destruction. I remember now nothing that I saw except the burning of vast quantities of cotton packed in bales, and that I was greatly astonished to see how slowly it burned.

On the afternoon of the 15th I joined Grant again at his headquarters at Clinton. Early the next morning we had definite information about Pemberton. He was about ten miles to the west, with twenty-five thousand men, as reported, and our advance was almost up with him. We at once went forward to the front. Here we found Pemberton in a most formidable position on the crest of a wooded ridge called Champion's Hill, over which the road passed longitudinally. About eleven o'clock in the morning of the 16th the battle began, and by four in the afternoon it was won.

After the battle I started out on horseback with Colonel Rawlins to visit the field. When we reached Logan's command we found him greatly excited. He declared the day was lost, and that he would soon be swept from his position. I contested the point with him. "Why, general," I said, "we have gained the day."

He could not see it. "Don't you hear the cannon over there?" he answered. "They will be down on us right away! In an hour I will have twenty thousand men to fight."

I found afterward that this was simply a curious idiosyncrasy of Logan's. In the beginning of a fight he was one of the bravest men that could be, saw no danger, went right on fighting until the battle was over. Then, after the battle was won, his mind gained an immovable conviction that it was lost. Where we were victorious, he thought that we were defeated. I had a very interesting conversation with Logan on this day, when he attempted to convince me that we had lost the battle of Champion's Hill. It was merely an intellectual peculiarity. It did not in the least impair his value as a soldier or commanding officer. He never made any mistake on account of it.

On leaving Logan, Rawlins and I were joined by several officers, and we continued our ride over the field. On the hill where the thickest of the fight had taken place we stopped, and were looking around at the dead and dying men lying all about us, when suddenly a man, perhaps forty-five or fifty years old, who had a Confederate uniform on, lifted himself up on his elbow, and said:

"For God's sake, gentlemen, is there a Mason among you?"

"Yes," said Rawlins, "I am a Mason." He got off his horse and kneeled by the dying man, who gave him some letters out of his pocket. When he came back Rawlins had tears on his cheeks. The man, he told us, wanted him to convey some souvenir—a miniature or a ring, I do not remember what—to his wife, who was in Alabama. Rawlins took the package, and sometime afterward he succeeded in sending it to the woman.

I remained out late that night conversing with the officers who had been in the battle, and think it must have been about eleven o'clock when I got to Grant's headquarters, where I was to sleep. Two or three officers who had been out with me went with me into the little cottage which Grant had taken possession of. We found a wounded man there, a tall and fine-looking man, a Confederate. He stood up suddenly and said: "Kill me! Will someone kill me? I am in such anguish that it will be mercy to do it—I have got to die—kill me—don't let me suffer!" We sent for a surgeon, who examined his case, but said it was hopeless. He had been shot through the head, so that it had cut off the optic nerve of both eyes. He never could possibly see again. Before morning he died.

I was up at daylight the next day, and off with Grant and his staff after the enemy. We rode directly west, and overtook Pemberton at the Big Black. He had made a stand on the bottom lands at the east head of the Big Black bridge. Here he fought in rifle-pits, protected by abatis and a difficult bayou. Lawler's brigade, of McClernand's corps, charged the left of the Confederate rifle-pits magnificently, taking more prisoners than their own numbers. The others fled. Pemberton burned his bridge and retreated rapidly into Vicksburg, with only three cannon out of sixty-three with which he had entered upon this short, sharp, and decisive campaign.

There was nothing for Grant to do now but build bridges and follow. Before morning four bridges had been thrown across the Big Black, and by the evening of that day, the 18th, the army had arrived behind Vicksburg, which was now its front. In twenty-four hours after Grant's arrival the town was invested, the bluffs above the town had been seized so that we could get water from the Mississippi, and Haynes's Bluff up the Yazoo had been abandoned by the Confederates. With the Yazoo highlands in our control there was no difficulty in establishing a line of supplies with our original base on the Mississippi. On the 20th I was able to get off to Mr. Stanton the first dispatch from the rear of Vicksburg. In it I said, "Probably the town will be carried today."

The prediction was not verified. The assault we expected was not made until the morning of the 22d. It failed, but without heavy loss. Early in the afternoon, however, McClernand, who was on the left of our lines, reported that he was in possession of two forts of the rebel line, was hard pressed, and in great need of re-enforcements. Not doubting that he had really succeeded in taking and holding the works he pretended to hold, General

Grant sent a division to his support, and at the same time ordered Sherman and McPherson to make new attacks. McClernand's report was false, for, although a few of his men had broken through in one place, he had not taken a single fort, and the result of the second assault was disastrous. We were repulsed, losing quite heavily, when but for his error the total loss of the day would have been inconsiderable.

The failure of the 22d convinced Grant of the necessity of a regular siege, and immediately the army settled down to that. We were in an incomparable position for a siege as regarded the health and comfort of our men. The high wooded hills afforded pure air and shade, and the deep ravines abounded in springs of excellent water, and if they failed it was easy to bring it from the Mississippi. Our line of supplies was beyond the reach of the enemy, and there was an abundance of fruit all about us. I frequently met soldiers coming into camp with buckets full of mulberries, blackberries, and red and yellow wild plums.

The army was deployed at this time in the following way: The right of the besieging force was held by General Sherman, whose forces ran from the river along the bluffs around the northeast of the town. Sherman's front was at a greater distance from the enemy than that of any other corps, and the approach less advantageous, but he began his siege works with great energy and admirable skill. Everything I saw of Sherman at the Vicksburg siege increased my admiration for him. He was a very brilliant man and an excellent commander of a corps. Sherman's information was great, and he was a clever talker. He always liked to have people about who could keep up with his conversation; besides, he was genial and unaffected. I particularly admired his loyalty to Grant. He had criticized the plan of campaign frankly in the first place, but had supported every movement with all his energy, and now that we were in the rear of Vicksburg he gave loud praise to the commander in chief.

To the left of Sherman lay the Seventeenth Army Corps, under Major-General [James Birdseye] McPherson [killed July, 1864]. He was one of the best officers we had. He was but thirty-two years old at the time, and a very handsome, gallant looking man, with rather a dark complexion, dark eyes, and a most cordial manner. McPherson was an engineer officer of fine natural ability and extraordinary acquirements, having graduated Number One in his class at West Point, and was held in high estimation by Grant and his professional brethren. Halleck gave him his start in the civil war, and he had been with Grant at Donelson and ever since. He was a man without any pretensions, and always had a pleasant handshake for you.

It is a little remarkable that the three chief figures in this great Vicksburg campaign—Grant, Sherman, and McPherson—were all born in Ohio. The utmost cordiality and confidence existed between these three men, and it always seemed to me that much of the success achieved in these marches and battles was owing to this very fact. There was no jealousy or bickering, and in their unpretending simplicity they were as alike as three peas. No country was ever more faithfully, unselfishly served than was ours in the Vicksburg campaign by these three Ohio officers.

To McPherson's left was the Thirteenth Army Corps, under Major-General John A. McClernand. Next to Grant he was the ranking officer in the army.

The approaches on his front were most favorable to us, and the enemy's line of works evidently much the weakest there, but he was very inefficient and slow in pushing his siege operations. Grant had resolved on the 23d to relieve McClernand for his false dispatch of the day before stating that he held two of the enemy's forts, but he changed his mind, concluding that it would be better on the whole to leave him in his command till the siege was concluded. From the time that I had joined Grant's army at Milliken's Bend and heard him criticizing Porter, Sherman, and other officers, I had been observing McClernand narrowly myself. My own judgment of him by this time was that he had not the qualities necessary for commander even of a regiment. In the first place, he was not a military man; he was a politician and a member of Congress. He was a man of a good deal of a certain kind of talent, not of a high order, but not one of intellectual accomplishments. His education was that which a man gets who is in Congress five or six years. In short, McClernand was merely a smart man, quick, very active-minded, but his judgment was not solid, and he looked after himself a good deal. Mr. Lincoln also looked out carefully for McClernand, because he was an Illinois Democrat, with a considerable following among the people. It was a great thing to get McClernand into the war in the first place, for his natural predisposition, one would have supposed, would have been to sympathize with the South. As long as he adhered to the war he carried his Illinois constituency with him; and chiefly for this reason, doubtless, Lincoln made it a point to take special care of him. In doing this the President really served the greater good of the cause. But from the circumstances of Lincoln's supposed friendship, McClernand had more consequence in the army than he deserved.

SOME CONTEMPORARY PORTRAITS

Living at headquarters as I did throughout the siege of Vicksburg, I soon became intimate with General Grant, not only knowing every operation while it was still but an idea, but studying its execution on the spot. Grant was an uncommon fellow—the most modest, the most disinterested, and the most honest man I ever knew, with a temper that nothing could disturb, and a judgment that was judicial in its comprehensiveness and wisdom. Not a great man, except morally; not an original or brilliant man, but sincere, thoughtful, deep, and gifted with courage that never faltered; when the time came to risk all, he went in like a simple-hearted, unaffected, unpretending hero, whom no ill omens could deject and no triumph unduly exalt. A social, friendly man, too, fond of a pleasant joke and also ready with one; but liking above all a long chat of an evening, and ready to sit up with you all night, talking in the cool breeze in front of his tent. Not a man of sentimentality, not demonstrative in friendship, but always holding to his friends, and just even to the enemies he hated.

After Grant, I spent more time at Vicksburg with his assistant adjutant general, Colonel John A. Rawlins, and with Lieutenant-Colonel Wilson, than with anybody else. Rawlins was one of the most valuable men in the army, in my judgment.

Wilson wrote the only biography of Rawlins and called him, "all things considered, ... the most remarkable man I met during the Civil War. Before his death from tuberculosis, Rawlins served as Grant's Secretary of War. Wilson was quite unhappy with the lack of credit given Rawlins in Grant's memoirs.—Ed. 2018

He had but a limited education, which he had picked up at the neighborhood school and in Galena, Ill., near which place he was born and where he had worked himself into the law; but he had a very able mind, clear, strong, and not subject to hysterics. He bossed everything at Grant's headquarters. He had very little respect for persons, and a rough style of conversation. I have heard him curse at Grant when, according to his judgment, the general was doing something that he thought he had better not do. But he was entirely devoted to his duty, with the clearest judgment, and perfectly fearless. Without him Grant would not have been the same man. Rawlins was essentially a good man, though he was one of the most profane men I ever knew; there was no guile in him—he was as upright and as genuine a character as I ever came across.

James H. Wilson I had first met at Milliken's Bend, when he was serving as chief topographical engineer and assistant inspector general of the Army of the Tennessee. He was a brilliant man intellectually, highly educated, and thoroughly companionable. We became warm friends at once, and were together a great deal throughout the war. Rarely did Wilson go out on a specially interesting tour of inspection that he did not invite me to accompany him, and I never failed, if I were at liberty, to accept his invitations. Much of the exact information about the condition of the works which I was able to send to Mr. Stanton Wilson put in my way.

I have already spoken of McClernand, Sherman, and McPherson, Grant's three chief officers, but there were many subordinate officers of value in his army, not a few of whom became afterward soldiers of distinction. At the request of Secretary Stanton, I had begun at Vicksburg a series of semi-official letters, in which I undertook to give my impressions of the officers in Grant's army. These letters were designed to help Mr. Lincoln and Mr. Stanton in forming their judgments of the men. In order to set the personnel of the commanding force distinctly before the reader, I quote here one of these letters, written at Cairo after the siege had ended. It has never been published before, and it gives my judgment at that time of the subordinate officers in the Vicksburg campaign:

Cairo, Ill., July 12, 1863.

Dear Sir: Your dispatch of June 29th, desiring me to "continue my sketches," I have today seen for the first time. It was sent down the river, but had not arrived when I left Vicksburg on the 5th instant.

Let me describe the generals of division and brigade in Grant's army in the order of the army corps to which they are attached, beginning with the Thirteenth.

The most prominent officer of the Thirteenth Corps, next to the commander of the corps, is Brigadier-General A. P. Hovey. He is a lawyer of Indiana, and from forty to forty-five years old. He is ambitious, active, nervous, irritable, energetic, clear-headed, quick-witted, and prompt-handed. He works with all his might and all his mind; and, unlike most volunteer officers, makes it his business to learn the military profession just as if he expected to spend his life in it. He distinguished himself most honorably at Port Gibson and Champion's Hill, and is one of the best officers in this army. He is a man whose character will always command respect, though he is too anxious about his personal renown and his own advancement to be considered a first-rate man morally, judged by the high standard of men like Grant and Sherman.

Hovey's principal brigadiers are General McGinnis and Colonel Slack. McGinnis is brave enough, but too excitable. He lost his balance at Champion's Hill. He is not likely ever to be more than a brigadier. Slack is a solid, steady man, brave, thorough, and sensible, but will never set the river afire. His education is poor, but he would make a respectable brigadier general, and, I know, hopes to be promoted.

Next to Hovey is Osterhaus. This general is universally well spoken of. He is a pleasant, genial fellow, brave and quick, and makes a first-rate report of a reconnaissance. There is not another general in this army who keeps the commander in chief so well informed concerning whatever happens at his outposts. As a disciplinarian he is not equal to Hovey, but is much better than some others. On the battlefield he lacks energy and concentrativeness. His brigade commanders are all colonels, and I don't know much of them.

The third division of the Thirteenth Corps is commanded by General A. J. Smith, an old cavalry officer of the regular service. He is intrepid to recklessness, his head is clear though rather thick, his disposition honest and manly, though given to boasting and self-exaggeration of a gentle and innocent kind. His division is well cared for, but is rather famous for slow instead of rapid marching. McClernand, however, disliked him, and kept him in the rear throughout the late campaign. He is a good officer to command a division in an army corps, but should not be entrusted with any important independent command.

Smith's principal brigadier is General Burbridge, whom I judge to be a mediocre officer, brave, rather pretentious, a good fellow, not destined to greatness.

The fourth division in the Thirteenth Corps is General Carr's. He has really been sick throughout the campaign, and had leave to go home several weeks since, but stuck it out till the surrender. This may account for a critical, hang-back disposition which he has several times exhibited. He is a man of more cultivation, intelligence, and thought than his colleagues generally. The discipline in his camps I have thought to be poor and careless. He is brave enough, but lacks energy and initiative.

Carr's brigadiers comprise General M[ichael] K. Lawler and General Lee, of Kansas. Lawler weighs two hundred and fifty pounds, is a Roman Catholic, and was a Douglas Democrat, belongs in Shawneetown, Ill., and served in the Mexican War. He is as brave as a lion, and has about as much brains; but his purpose is always honest, and his sense is always good. He is a good disciplinarian and a first-rate soldier. He once hung a man of his regiment for murdering a comrade, without reporting the case to his commanding general either before or after the hanging, but there was no doubt the man deserved his fate. Grant has two or three times gently reprimanded him for indiscretions, but is pretty sure to go and thank him after a battle. Carr's third brigadier I don't know.

Grant, during the Chattanooga campaign, while praising several Illinois generals, said, "But when it comes to just plain hard fighting I would rather trust Old Mike Lawler than any of them."

In the Fifteenth Corps there are two major generals who command divisions—namely, Steele and Blair—and one brigadier, Tuttle. Steele has also been sick through the campaign, but has kept constantly at his post. He is a gentlemanly, pleasant fellow. . . . Sherman has a high opinion of his capacity, and everyone says that he handles troops with great coolness and skill in battle. To me his mind seems to work in a desultory way, like the mind of a captain of infantry long habituated to garrison duty at a frontier post. He takes things in bits, like a gossiping companion, and never comprehensively and strongly, like a man of clear brain and a ruling purpose. But on the whole I consider him one of the best division generals in this army, yet you cannot rely on him to make a logical statement, or to exercise any independent command.

Of Steele's brigadiers, Colonel Woods eminently deserves promotion. A Hercules in form, in energy, and in pertinacity, he is both safe and sure. Colonel Manter, of Missouri, is a respectable officer. General Thayer is a fair but not first-rate officer.

Frank Blair is about the same as an officer that he is as a politician. He is intelligent, prompt, determined, rather inclining to disorder, a poor disciplinarian, but a brave fighter. I judge that he will soon leave the army, and that he prefers his seat in Congress to his commission.

Frank and his brother both served. The family was close to Lincoln and their father's house on Lafayette Square near the White House still stands.—Ed. 2018

In Frank Blair's division there are two brigadier generals, Ewing and Lightburne. Ewing seems to possess many of the qualities of his father, whom you know better than I do, I suppose. Lightburne has not served long with this army, and I have had no opportunity of learning his measure. Placed in a command during the siege where General Sherman himself directed what was to be done, he has had little to do. He seems to belong to the heavy rather than the rapid department of the forces.

Colonel Giles Smith is one of the very best brigadiers in Sherman's corps, perhaps the best of all next to Colonel Woods.

He only requires the chance to develop into an officer of uncommon power and usefulness. There are plenty of men with generals' commissions who in all military respects are not fit to tie his shoes.

Of General Tuttle, who commands Sherman's third division, I have already spoken, and need not here repeat it. Bravery and zeal constitute his only qualifications for command. His principal brigadier is General Mower, a brilliant officer, but not of large mental calibre. Colonel Wood, who commands another of his brigades, is greatly esteemed by General Grant, but I do not know him; neither do I know the commander of his third brigade.

Three divisions of the Sixteenth Corps have been serving in Grant's army for some time past. They are all commanded by brigadier generals, and the brigades by colonels. The first of these divisions to arrive before Vicksburg was Lauman's. This general got his promotion by bravery on the field and Iowa political influence. He is totally unfit to command—a very good man but a very poor general. His brigade commanders are none of them above mediocrity. The next division of the Sixteenth Corps to join the Vicksburg army was General Kimball's. He is not so bad a commander as Lauman, but he is bad enough; brave, of course, but lacking the military instinct and the genius of generalship. I don't know any of his brigade commanders. The third division of the Sixteenth Corps now near Vicksburg is that of General W. S. Smith. He is one of the best officers in that army. A rigid disciplinarian, his division is always ready and always safe. A man of brains, a hard worker, unpretending, quick, suggestive, he may also be a little crotchety, for such is his reputation; but I judge that he only needs the opportunity to render great services. What his brigade commanders are worth I can't say, but I am sure they have a first-rate schoolmaster in him.

I now come to the Seventeenth Corps and to its most prominent division general, Logan. This is a man of remarkable qualities and peculiar character. Heroic and brilliant, he is sometimes unsteady. Inspiring his men with his own enthusiasm on the field of battle, he is splendid in all its crash and commotion, but before it begins he is doubtful of the result, and after it is over he is fearful we may yet be beaten. A man of instinct and not of reflection, his judgments are often absurd, but his extemporaneous opinions are very apt to be right. Deficient in education, he is full of generous attachments and sincere animosities. On the whole, few can serve the cause of the country more effectively than he, and none serve it more faithfully.

John Alexander Logan (1826 – 1886) was a soldier and political leader. He and his wife were for decades fixtures in Washington social life. See A Soldier's Wife at the Center of National Life.—Ed. 2018

Logan's oldest brigade commander is General John D. Stevenson, of Missouri. He is a person of much talent, but a grumbler. He was one of the oldest colonels in the volunteer service, but because he had always been an antislavery man all the others were promoted before him. This is still one of his grounds for discontent, and in addition younger brigadiers have been put before him since. Thus the world will not go to suit him. He has his own notions, too, of what should be done on the field of battle, and General McPherson has twice during this campaign had to rebuke him very severely for his failure to come to time on critical occasions.

Logan's second brigade is commanded by General Leggett, of Ohio. This officer has distinguished himself during the siege, and will be likely to distinguish himself hereafter. He possesses a clear head, an equable temper, and great propulsive power over his men. He is also a hard worker, and whatever he touches goes easily. The third brigade of this division has for a short time been commanded by Colonel Force. I only know that Logan, McPherson, and Grant all think well of him.

Next in rank among McPherson's division generals is McArthur. He has been in the reserve throughout the campaign, and has had little opportunity of proving his mettle. He is a shrewd, steady Scotchman, trustworthy rather than brilliant, good at hard knocks, but not a great commander. Two of his brigadiers, however, have gained very honorable distinction in this campaign, namely Crocker, who commanded Quinby's division at

Port Gibson, Raymond, Jackson, and Champion's Hill, and Ransom. Crocker was sick throughout, and, as soon as Quinby returned to his command, had to go away, and it is feared may never be able to come back. He is an officer of great promise and remarkable power. Ransom has commanded on McPherson's right during the siege, and has exceeded every other brigadier in the zeal, intelligence, and efficiency with which his siege works were constructed and pushed forward. At the time of the surrender his trenches were so well completed that the engineers agreed that they offered the best opportunity in the whole of our lines for the advance of storming columns. Captain Comstock told me that ten thousand men could there be marched under cover up to the very lines of the enemy. In the assault of May 22d, Ransom was equally conspicuous for the bravery with which he exposed himself. No young man in all this army has more future than he.

The third brigade of McArthur's division, that of General Reid, has been detached during the campaign at Lake Providence and elsewhere, and I have not been able to make General R.'s acquaintance.

The third division of the Seventeenth Corps was commanded during the first of the siege by General Quinby. This officer was also sick, and I dare say did not do justice to himself. A good commander of a division he is not, though he is a most excellent and estimable man, and seemed to be regarded by the Soldiers with much affection. But he lacks order, system, command, and is the very opposite of his successor, General John E. Smith, who, with much less intellect than Quinby, has a great deal better sense, with a firmness of character, a steadiness of hand, and a freedom from personal irritability and jealousy which must soon produce the happiest effect upon the division. Smith combines with these natural qualities of a soldier and commander a conscientious devotion not merely to the doing but also to the learning of his duty, which renders him a better and better general every day. He is also fit to be entrusted with any independent command where judgment and discretion are as necessary as courage and activity, for in him all these qualities seem to be happily blended and balanced.

Of General Matthias, who commands the brigade in this division so long and so gallantly commanded by the late Colonel Boomer, I hear the best accounts, but do not know him personally. The medical inspector tells me that no camps in the lines are kept in so good condition as his; and General Sherman, under whom he lately served, speaks of him as a very valuable officer. The second brigade is commanded by Colonel Sanborn, a steady, mediocre sort of man; the third by Colonel Holmes, whom I don't know personally, but who made a noble fight at Champion's Hill, and saved our center there from being broken.

General Herron's division is the newest addition to the forces under Grant, except the Ninth Corps, of which I know nothing except that its discipline and organization exceed those of the Western troops. Herron is a driving, energetic sort of young fellow, not deficient either in self-esteem or in common sense, and, as I judge, hardly destined to distinctions higher than those he has already acquired. Of his two brigadiers, Vandever has not proved himself of much account during the siege; Orme I have seen, but do not know. Herron has shown a great deal more both of capacity and force than either of them. But he has not the first great requisite of a soldier, obedience to orders, and believes too much in doing things his own way. Thus, for ten days after he had taken his position he disregarded the order properly to picket the bottom between the bluff and the river on his left. He had made up his own mind that nobody could get out of the town by that way, and accordingly neglected to have the place thoroughly examined in order to render the matter clear and certain. Presently Grant discovered that men from the town were making their escape through that bottom, and then a more peremptory command to Herron set the matter right by the establishment of the necessary pickets.

I must not omit a general who formerly commanded a brigade in Logan's division, and has for some time been detached to a separate command at Milliken's Bend. I mean General Dennis.

He is a hard-headed, hard-working, conscientious man, who never knows when he is beaten, and consequently is very hard to beat. He is not brilliant, but safe, sound, and trustworthy. His predecessor in that command, General Sullivan, has for some time been at Grant's headquarters, doing nothing with more energy and effect than he would be likely to show in any other line of duty. He is a gentlemanly fellow, intelligent, a charming companion, but heavy, jovial, and lazy.

I might write another letter on the staff officers and staff organization of Grant's army, should you desire it.

Yours faithfully,

C. A. Dana.

The day after sending to Mr. Stanton this letter on the generals of divisions and of brigades in the army which besieged Vicksburg, I wrote him another on the staff officers of the various corps. Like its predecessor, this letter has never appeared in the records of the war:

Cairo, Ill., July 13, 1863.

Dear Sir: In my letter of yesterday I accidentally omitted to notice General C. C. Washburn among the generals of division in Grant's army. He is now in command of two of the divisions detached from the Sixteenth Army Corps—namely, that of Kimball and that of W. S. Smith—and, as I happen to know, is anxious to be put in command of an army corps, for which purpose it has been suggested that a new corps might be created out of these two divisions, with the addition of that of Lauman, also detached from the Sixteenth, or that of Herron. But I understand from General Grant that he is not favorable to any such arrangement. Washburn being one of the very youngest in rank of his major generals, he intends to put him in command of a single division as soon as possible, in order that he may prove his fitness for higher commands by actual service, and give no occasion for older soldiers to complain that he is promoted without regard to his merits.

I know Washburn very well, both as a politician and -a military man, and I say frankly that he has better qualities for the latter than for the former function. He is brave, steady, respectable; receives suggestions and weighs them carefully; is not above being advised, but acts with independence nevertheless. His judgment is good, and his vigilance sufficient. I have not seen him in battle, however, and cannot say how far he holds his mind there. I don't find in him, I am sorry to say, that effort to learn the military art which every commander ought to exhibit, no matter whether he has received a military education or not. Washburn's whole soul is not put into the business of arms, and for me that is an unpardonable defect. But he is a good man, and above the average of our generals, at least of those in Grant's command.

I now come to the staff organization and staff officers of this army, beginning, of course, with those connected with the head of the department. Grant's staff is a curious mixture of good, bad, and indifferent. As he is neither an organizer nor a disciplinarian himself, his staff is naturally a mosaic of accidental elements and family friends. It contains four working men, two who are able to accomplish their duties without much work, and several who either don't think of work, or who accomplish nothing no matter what they undertake.

Lieutenant-Colonel Rawlins, Grant's assistant adjutant general, is a very industrious, conscientious man, who never loses a moment, and never gives himself any indulgence except swearing and scolding. He is a lawyer by profession, a townsman of Grant's, and has a great influence over him, especially because he watches him day and night, and whenever he commits the folly of tasting liquor hastens to remind him that at the beginning of the war he gave him [Rawlins] his word of honor not to touch a drop as long as it lasted. Grant thinks Rawlins a first-rate adjutant, but I think this is a mistake. He is too slow, and can't write the English language correctly without a great deal of careful consideration. Indeed, illiterateness is a general characteristic of Grant's staff, and in fact of Grant's generals and regimental officers of all ranks.

Major Bowers, judge-advocate of Grant's staff, is an excellent man, and always finds work to do. Lieutenant-Colonel Wilson, inspector general, is a person of similar disposition. He is a captain of engineers in the regular army, and has rendered valuable services in that capacity. The fortifications of Haynes's Bluff were designed by him and executed under his direction. His leading idea is the idea of duty, and he applies it vigorously and often impatiently to others. In consequence he is unpopular among all who like to live with little work. But he has remarkable talents and uncommon executive power, and will be heard from hereafter.

The quartermaster's department is under charge of Lieutenant-Colonel Bingham, who is one of those I spoke of as accomplishing much with little work. He is an invalid almost, and I have never seen him when he appeared to be perfectly well; but he is a man of first-rate abilities and solid character, and, barring physical weakness, up to even greater responsibilities than those he now bears.

The chief commissary, Lieutenant-Colonel Macfeely, is a jolly, agreeable fellow, who never seems to be at work, but I have heard no complaints of deficiencies in his department. On the contrary, it seems to be one of the most efficacious parts of this great machine.

Lieutenant-Colonel Kent, provost-marshal general, is a very industrious and sensible man, a great improvement on his predecessor, Colonel Hillyer, who was a family and personal friend of Grant's.

There are two aides-de-camp with the rank of colonel, namely, Colonel— and Colonel—, both personal friends of Grant's.— is a worthless, whisky-drinking, useless fellow.— is decent and gentlemanly, but neither of them is worth his salt so far as service to the Government goes. Indeed, in all my observation, I have never discovered the use of Grant's aides-de-camp at all. On the battlefield he sometimes sends orders by them, but everywhere else they are idle loafers. I suppose the army would be better off if they were all suppressed, especially the colonels.

Grant has three aides with the rank of captain. Captain— is a relative of Mrs. Grant. He has been a stage driver, and violates English grammar at every phrase. He is of some use, for he attends to the mails.

Captain— is an elegant young officer of the regular cavalry. He rides after the general when he rides out; the rest of the time he does nothing at all. Captain [Adam] Badeau, wounded at Port Hudson since he was attached to Grant's staff, has not yet reported.

While writing his memoirs in 1885, in hopes they would sustain his family after his approaching death from cancer, Grant signed an agreement with Badeau for assistance in editing the work. Before completion, Badeau complained that he should be paid more up front and from the royalties. The two severed relations and Badeau sued. He later came to an agreement with Julia Grant after the general's death.—Ed. 2018

I must not omit the general medical staff of this army. It is in bad order. Its head, Dr. Mills, is impracticable, earnest, quarrelsome. He was relieved several weeks since, but Grant likes him, and kept him on till the fall of Vicksburg. In this he was right, no doubt, for a change during the siege would have been troublesome. The change, I presume, will now be made. It must be for the better.

The office of chief of artillery on the general staff I had forgotten, as well as that of chief engineer. The former is occupied by Lieutenant-Colonel Duff, of the Second Illinois Artillery. He is unequal to the position, not only because he is disqualified by sickness, but because he does not sufficiently understand the management of artillery. The siege suffered greatly from his incompetence. General Grant knows, of course, that he is not the right person; but it is one of his weaknesses that he is unwilling to hurt the feelings of a friend, and so he keeps him on.

The chief engineer, Captain Comstock, is an officer of great merit. He has, too, what his predecessor, Captain Prime, lacked, a talent for organization. His accession to the army will be the source of much improvement.

If General Grant had about him a staff of thoroughly competent men, disciplinarians and workers, the efficiency and fighting quality of his army would soon be much increased. As it is, things go too much by hazard and by spasms; or, when the pinch comes, Grant forces through, by his own energy and main strength, what proper organization and proper staff officers would have done already.

The staff of the Thirteenth Corps was formed by General McClernand. The acting adjutant general, Lieutenant-Colonel Scates, is a man of about fifty-five or sixty years old; he was a judge in Illinois, and left an honored and influential social position to serve in the army. General Ord speaks in high terms of him as an officer. The chief of artillery, Colonel —, is an ass.

The chief quartermaster, Lieutenant-Colonel—, General McClernand's father-in-law, lately resigned his commission. He was incompetent. . . . His successor has not yet been appointed. The chief commissary, Lieutenant-Colonel—, is a fussy fellow, who with much show accomplishes but little. General McClernand's aides went away with him or are absent on leave. Not a man of them is worth having. The engineer on his staff, Lieutenant Hains, is an industrious and useful officer. The medical director, Dr. Hammond, had just been appointed.

In the Fifteenth Corps staff all have to be working men, for Sherman tolerates no idlers and finds something for everybody to do. If an officer proves unfit for his position, he shifts him to some other place. Thus his adjutant, Lieutenant-Colonel Hammond, a restless Kentuckian, kept everything in a row as long as he remained in that office. Sherman has accordingly made him inspector general, and during the last two months has kept him constantly employed on scouting parties. In his place as adjutant is Captain Sawyer, a quiet, industrious, efficient person. The chief of artillery, Major Taylor, directed by Sherman's omnipresent eye and quick judgment, is an officer of great value, though under another general he might not be worth so much. The chief engineer, Captain Pitzman, wounded about July 15th, is a man of merit, and his departure was a great loss to the regular ranks. General Sherman has three aides-de-camp, Captain McCoy, Captain Dayton, and Lieutenant Hill, and, as I have said, neither of them holds a sinecure office. His medical director, Dr. McMillan, is a good physician, I believe; he has been in a constant contention with Dr. Mills. The quartermaster, Lieutenant-Colonel J. C. Smith, is a most efficient officer; he has been doing duty as commissary also.

On the whole, General Sherman has a very small and very efficient staff; but the efficiency comes mainly from him. What a splendid soldier he is!

The staff of the Seventeenth Army Corps is the most complete, the most numerous, and in some respects the most serviceable in this army.

The adjutant general, Lieutenant-Colonel Clark, is a person of uncommon quickness, is always at work, and keeps everything in his department in first-rate order. The inspector general, Lieutenant-Colonel Strong, does his duties with promptness and thoroughness; his reports are models. The chief of artillery, Lieutenant-Colonel Powell, thoroughly understands his business, and attends to it diligently. The provost-marshal general, Lieutenant-Colonel Wilson, is a judicious and industrious man. Both the quartermaster and commissary are new men, captains, and I do not know them, but McPherson speaks highly of them. The medical director, Dr. Boucher, has the reputation of keeping his hospitals in better order and making his reports more promptly and satisfactorily than any other medical officer in this army. General McPherson has four aides-de-camp: Captain Steele, Captain Gile, Lieutenant Knox, and Lieutenant Vernay. The last of these is the best, and Captain Steele is next to him. The engineer officer, Captain Hickenlooper, is a laborious man, quick, watchful, but not of great capacity. The picket officer, Major Willard, whom I accidentally name last, is a person of unusual merit.

In the staffs of the division and brigadier generals I do not now recall any officer of extraordinary capacity. There may be such, but I have not made their acquaintance. On the other hand, I have made the acquaintance of some who seemed quite unfit for their places. I must not omit, however, to speak here of Captain Tresilian, engineer on the staff of Major-General Logan. His general services during the siege were not conspicuous, but he deserves great credit for constructing the wooden mortars which General McPherson used near its close with most remarkable effect. Both the idea and the work were Tresilian's.

Very possibly you may not wish to go through this mass of details respecting so many officers of inferior grades, upon whose claims you may never be called to pass judgment. But if you care to read them here they are. I remain, dear sir,

Yours very faithfully,

C. A. Dana.

THE SIEGE OF VICKSBURG

We had not been many days in the rear of Vicksburg before we settled into regular habits. The men were detailed in reliefs for work in the trenches, and being relieved at fixed hours everybody seemed to lead a systematic life.

My chief duty throughout the siege was a daily round through the trenches, generally with the corps commander or some one of his staff. As the lines of investment were six or seven miles long, it occupied the greater part of my day; sometimes I made a portion of my tour of inspection in the night. One night in riding through the trenches I must have passed twenty thousand men asleep on their guns. I still can see the grotesque positions into which they had curled themselves. The trenches were so protected that there was no danger in riding through them. It was not so safe to venture on the hills overlooking Vicksburg. I went on foot and alone one day to the top of a hill, and was looking at the town, when I suddenly heard something go whizz, whizz, by my ear. "What in the world is that?" I asked myself. The place was so desolate that it was an instant before I could believe that these were bullets intended for me. When I did realize it, I immediately started to lie down. Then came the question, which was the best way to lie down. If I lay at right angles to the enemy's line the bullets from the right and left might strike me; if I lay parallel to it then those directly from the front might hit me. So I concluded it made no difference which way I lay. After remaining quiet for a time the bullets ceased, and I left the hill-top. I was more cautious in the future in venturing beyond cover.

Through the entire siege I lived in General Grant's headquarters, which were on a high bluff northeast of Sherman's extreme left. I had a tent to myself, and on the whole was very comfortable. We never lacked an abundance of provisions. There was good water, enough even for the bath, and we suffered very little from excessive heat. The only serious annoyance was the cannonade from our whole line, which from the first of June went on steadily by night as well as by day. The following bit from a letter I wrote on June 2d, to my little daughter, tells something of my situation:

> It is real summer weather here, and, after coming in at noon today from my usual ride through the trenches, I was very glad to get a cold bath in my tent before dinner. I like living in tents very well, especially if you ride on horseback all day. Every night I sleep with one side of the tent wide open and the walls put up all around to get plenty of air. Sometimes I wake up in the night and think it is raining, the wind roars so in the tops of the great oak forest on the hillside where we are encamped, and I think it is thundering till I look out and see the golden moonlight in all its glory, and listen again and know that it is only the thunder of General Sherman's great guns, that neither rest nor let others rest by night or by day.

We were no sooner in position behind Vicksburg than Grant saw that he must have reinforcements. Joe Johnston was hovering near, working with energy to collect forces sufficient to warrant an attempt to relieve Vicksburg. The Confederates were also known to be reorganizing at Jackson. Johnston eventually gathered an army behind Grant of about twenty-five thousand men.

Under these threatening circumstances it was necessary to keep a certain number of troops in our rear, more than Grant could well spare from the siege, and he therefore made every effort to secure reinforcements. He ordered down from Tennessee, and elsewhere in his own department, all available forces. He also sent to General Banks, who was then besieging Port Hudson, a request to bring his forces up as promptly as practicable, and assuring him that he (Grant) would gladly serve under him as his senior in rank, or simply cooperate with him for the benefit of the common cause, if Banks preferred that arrangement. To Halleck, on May 29th, he telegraphed: "If Banks does not come to my assistance I must be reinforced from elsewhere. I will avoid a surprise, and do the best I can with the means at hand." This was about the extent of Grant's personal appeals to his superiors for additional forces. No doubt, however, he left a good deal to my representations.

As no reply came from Banks, I started myself on the 30th for Port Hudson at Grant's desire, to urge that the reinforcements be furnished.

The route used for getting out from the rear of Vicksburg at that time was through the Chickasaw Bayou into the Yazoo and thence into the Mississippi. From the mouth of the Yazoo I crossed the Mississippi to Young's Point, and from there went overland across the peninsula to get a gunboat at a point south of Vicksburg. As we were going down the river we met a steamer just above Grand Gulf bearing one of the previous messengers whom Grant had sent to Banks. He was bringing word that Banks could send no forces; on the other hand, he asked reinforcements from Grant to aid in his siege of Port Hudson, which he had closely invested. This news, of course, made my trip unnecessary, and I returned at once to headquarters, having been gone not over twenty-four hours.

As soon as this news came from Banks, I sent an urgent appeal to Mr. Stanton to hurry reinforcements sufficient to make success beyond all peradventure. The Government was not slow to appreciate Grant's needs or the great opportunity he had created. Early in June I received the following dispatch from Mr. Stanton:

War Department, June 5, 1863.

Your telegrams up to the 30th have been received. Everything in the power of this Government will be put forth to aid General Grant. The emergency is not underrated here. Your telegrams are a great obligation, and are looked for with deep interest. I cannot thank you as much as I feel for the service you are now rendering. You have been appointed an assistant adjutant general, with rank of major, with liberty to report to General Grant if he needs you. The appointment may be a protection to you. I shall expect daily reports if possible.

Edwin M. Stanton,

Secretary of War.

My appointment as assistant adjutant general was Stanton's own idea. He was by nature a very anxious man. When he perceived from my dispatches that I was going every day on expeditions into dangerous territory, he became alarmed lest I might be caught by the Confederates; for as I was a private citizen it would have been difficult to exchange me. If I were in the regular volunteer service as an assistant adjutant general, however, there would be no trouble about an exchange, hence my appointment.

The chief variations from my business of watching the siege behind Vicksburg were these trips I made to inspect the operations against the enemy, who was now trying to shut us in from the rear beyond the Big Black. His heaviest force was to the northeast. On June 6th the reports from Satartia, our advance up the Yazoo, were so unsatisfactory that Grant decided to examine the situation there himself. That morning he said to me at breakfast:

"Mr. Dana, I am going to Satartia today; would you like to go along?"

I said I would, and we were soon on horseback, riding with a cavalry guard to Haynes's Bluff, where we took a small steamer reserved for Grant's use and carrying his flag. Grant was ill and went to bed soon after he started. We had gone up the river to within two miles of Satartia, when we met two gunboats coming down. Seeing the general's flag, the officers in charge of the gunboats came aboard our steamer and asked where the general was going. I told them to Satartia.

"Why," said they, "it will not be safe. Kimball [our advance was under the charge of Brigadier-General Nathan Kimball, Third Division, Sixteenth Army Corps] has retreated from there, and is sending all his supplies to Haynes's Bluff. The enemy is probably in the town now."

I told them Grant was sick and asleep, and that I did not want to waken him. They insisted that it was unsafe to go on, and that I would better call the general. Finally I did so, but he was too sick to decide.

"I will leave it with you," he said. I immediately said we would go back to Haynes's Bluff, which we did.

The next morning Grant came out to breakfast fresh as a rose, clean shirt and all, quite himself. "Well, Mr. Dana," he said, "I suppose we are at Satartia now."

"No, general," I said, "we are at Haynes's Bluff." And I told him what had happened.

He did not complain, but as he was short of officers at that point he asked me to go with a party of cavalry toward Mechanicsburg to find if it were true, as reported, that Joe Johnston was advancing from Canton to the Big Black. We had a hard ride, not getting back to Vicksburg until the morning of the eighth. The country was like all the rest around Vicksburg, broken, wooded, unpopulous, with bad roads and few streams. It still had many cattle, but the corn was pretty thoroughly cleared out. We found that Johnston had not ' moved his main force as rumored, and that he could not move it without bringing all his supplies with him.

Throughout the siege an attack from Johnston continued to threaten Grant and to keep a part of our army busy. Almost every one of my dispatches to Mr. Stanton contained rumors of the movements of the Confederates, and the information was so uncertain that often what I reported one day had to be contradicted the next. About the 15th of June the movements of the enemy were so threatening that Grant issued an order extending Sherman's command so as to include Haynes's Bluff, and to send there the two divisions of the Ninth Corps under General Parke. These troops had just arrived from Kentucky, and Grant had intended to place them on the extreme left of our besieging line.

Although our spies brought in daily reports of forces of the enemy at different points between Yazoo City and Jackson, Johnston's plan did not develop opportunity until the 22d, when he was said to be crossing the Big Black north of Bridgeport. Sherman immediately started to meet him with about thirty thousand troops, including cavalry. Five brigades more were held in readiness to reinforce him if necessary. The country was scoured by Sherman in efforts to beat Johnston, but no trace of an enemy was found. It was, however, ascertained that he had not advanced, but was still near Canton. As there was no design to attack Johnston until Vicksburg was laid low, Sherman made his way to Bear Creek, northwest of Canton, where he could watch the Confederates, and there went into camp.

I went up there several times to visit him, and always came away enthusiastic over his qualities as a soldier. His amazing activity and vigilance pervaded his entire force. The country where he had encamped was exceedingly favorable for defense. He had occupied the commanding points, opened rifle-pits wherever they would add to his advantage, obstructed the cross-roads and most of the direct roads also, and ascertained every point where the Big Black could be forded between the line of Benton on the north and the line of railroads on the south. By his rapid movements, also, and by widely deploying on all the ridges and open headlands, Sherman produced the impression that his forces were ten times as numerous as they really were. Sherman remained in his camp on Bear Creek through the rest of the siege, in order to prevent any possible attack by Joe Johnston, the reports about whose movements continued to be contradictory and uncertain.

Another variation in my Vicksburg life was visiting Admiral Porter, who commanded the fleet which hemmed in the city on the river-side. Porter was a very active, courageous, fresh-minded man, and an experienced naval officer, and I enjoyed the visits I made to his fleet. His boats were pretty well scattered, for the Confederates west of the Mississippi were pressing in, and unless watched might manage to cross somewhere.

See Porter's memoir, Incidents and Anecdotes of the Civil War.—Ed. 2018

Seven of the gunboats were south of Vicksburg, one at Haynes's Bluff, one was at Chickasaw Bayou, one at Young's Point, one at Milliken's Bend, one at Lake Providence, one at Greenell, one at

Island Sixty-five, two were at White River, and so on, and several were always in motion. They guarded the river so completely that no hostile movement from the west ever succeeded, or was likely to do so.

The most serious attack from the west during the siege was that on June 7th, when a force of some two thousand Confederates engaged about a thousand negro troops defending Milliken's Bend. This engagement at Milliken's Bend became famous from the conduct of the colored troops. General E. S. Dennis, who saw the battle, told me that it was the hardest fought engagement he had ever seen. It was fought mainly hand to hand. After it was over many men were found dead with bayonet stabs, and others with their skulls broken open by butts of muskets. "It is impossible," said General Dennis, "for men to show greater gallantry than the negro troops in that fight."

The bravery of the blacks in the battle at Milliken's Bend completely revolutionized the sentiment of the army with regard to the employment of negro troops. I heard prominent officers who formerly in private had sneered at the idea of the negroes fighting express themselves after that as heartily in favor of it. Among the Confederates, however, the feeling was very different. All the reports which came to us showed that both citizens and soldiers on the Confederate side manifested great dismay at the idea of our arming negroes.

They said that such a policy was certain to be followed by insurrection with all its horrors.

Although the presence of Joe Johnston on the east, and the rumors of invasion by Kirby Smith from the west, compelled constant attention, the real work behind Vicksburg was always that of the siege. No amount of outside alarm loosened Grant's hold on the rebel stronghold. The siege went on steadily and effectively. By June 10th the expected reinforcements began to report. Grant soon had eighty-five thousand men around Vicksburg, and Pemberton's last hope was gone. The first troops to arrive were eight regiments under General [Francis J.] Herron. They came from Missouri, down the Mississippi to Young's Point, where they were debarked and marched across the peninsula, care being taken, of course, that the Confederate garrison at Vicksburg should see the whole march. The troops were then ferried across the Mississippi, and took a position south of Vicksburg between Lauman's troops and the Mississippi River, completely closing the lines, and thus finally rendering egress and ingress absolutely impossible. Herron took this position on June 13th. He went to work with so much energy that on the night of the 15th he was able to throw forward his lines on his left, making an advance of five hundred yards, and bringing his artillery and rifle-pits within two or three hundred yards of the enemy's lines.

Herron was a first-rate officer, and the only consummate dandy I ever saw in the army. He was always handsomely dressed; I believe he never went out without patent-leather boots on, and you would see him in the middle of a battle—well, I cannot say exactly that he went into battle with a lace pocket-handkerchief, but at all events he always displayed a clean white one. But these little vanities appeared not to detract from his usefulness. Herron had already proved his ability and fighting qualities at the battle of Prairie Grove, December 7, 1862.

Just as our reinforcements arrived we began to receive encouraging reports from within Vicksburg. Deserters said that the garrison was worn out and hungry; besides, the defense had for several days been conducted with extraordinary feebleness, which Grant thought was due to the deficiency of ammunition or to exhaustion and depression in the garrison, or to their retirement to an inner line of defense. The first and third of these causes no doubt operated to some extent, but the second we supposed to be the most influential. The deserters also said that fully one third of the garrison were in hospital, and that officers, as well as men, had begun to despair of relief from Johnston.

These reports from within the town, as well as the progress of the siege and the arrival of reinforcements, pointed so strongly to the speedy surrender of the place that I asked Mr. Stanton in my dispatch of June 14th to please inform me by telegram whether he wished me to go to General Rosecrans after the fall of Vicksburg or whether he had other orders for me.

The next day after this letter, however, the enemy laid aside his long-standing inactivity and opened violently with both artillery and musketry. Two mortars which the Confederates got into operation that day in front of General A. J. Smith particularly interested our generals. I remember going with a party of some twenty officers, including Sherman, Ord, McPherson, and Wilson, to the brow of a hill on McPherson's front to watch this battery with our field glasses. From where we were we could study the whole operation. We saw the shell start from the mortar, sail slowly through the air toward us, fall to the ground and explode, digging out a hole which looked like a crater. I remember one of these craters which must have been nine feet in diameter. As you watched a shell coming you could not tell whether it would fall a thousand feet away or by your side. Yet nobody budged. The men sat there on their horses, their reins loose, studying and discussing the work of the batteries, apparently indifferent to the danger. It was very interesting as a study of human steadiness.

By the middle of June our lines were so near the enemy's on Sherman's and McPherson's front that General Grant began to consider the project of another general assault as soon as McClernand's, Lauman's, and Herron's lines were brought up close. Accordingly, Sherman and McPherson were directed to hold their work until the others were up to them. Herron, of course, had not had time to advance, though since his arrival he had worked with great energy. Lauman had done little in the way of regular approaches. But the chief difficulty in the way was the backwardness of McClernand. His trenches were mere rifle-pits, three or four feet wide, and would allow neither the passage of artillery nor the assemblage of any considerable number of troops. His batteries were, with scarcely an exception, in the position they apparently had held when the siege was opened.

This obstacle to success was soon removed. On the 18th of June McClernand was relieved and General Ord was put into his place. The immediate occasion of McClernand's removal was a congratulatory address to the Thirteenth Corps which he had fulminated in May, and which first reached the besieging army in a copy of the Missouri Democrat. In this extraordinary address McClernand claimed for himself most of the glory of the campaign, reaffirmed that on May 22d he had held two rebel forts for several hours, and imputed to other officers and troops failure to support him in their possession, which must have resulted in the capture of the town, etc. Though this congratulatory address was the occasion of McClernand's removal, the real causes of it dated farther back. These causes, as I understood at the time, were his repeated disobedience of important orders, his general unfortunate mental disposition, and his palpable incompetence for the duties of his position. I learned in private conversation that in General Grant's judgment it was necessary that McClernand should be removed for the reason, above all, that his bad relations with other corps commanders, especially Sherman and McPherson, rendered it impossible that the chief command of the army should devolve upon him, as it would have done were General Grant disabled, without some pernicious consequence to the Union cause.

PEMBERTON'S SURRENDER

Two days after McClernand's removal General Grant attempted to settle the question whether he should make a further attempt to storm Vicksburg or leave its reduction to the regular progress of siege operations. To test what an assault would do, he began, at four o'clock on the morning of June 20th, an artillery attack, in which about two hundred cannon were engaged. During the attack no Confederates were visible, nor was any reply made to our artillery. Their musketry fire also amounted to nothing. Of course, some damage was done to the buildings of the town by our concentrated cannonade, but we could not tell whether their mills, foundry, or storehouses were destroyed. Their rifle-pits and defenses were little injured. At ten o'clock the cannonade ceased. It was evident that the probabilities of immediate success by assault would not compensate for the sacrifices.

After the artillery attack on the 20th, the next exciting incident of the siege was the springing of a mine by McPherson. Directly in front of his position the enemy had a great fort which was regarded as the key of their line. As soon as McPherson had got into position behind Vicksburg he had begun to run trenches toward this fort, under which he subsequently tunneled, hoping that by an explosion he would open it to our occupation. The mine was sprung about four o'clock on the afternoon of June 25th. It was charged with twelve hundred pounds of powder. The explosion was terrific, forming a crater fully thirty-five feet in diameter, but it did not open the fort. There still remained between the new ground which we had gained by the explosion and the main works of the fort an ascent so steep that an assault was practically impossible. The enemy very soon opened a galling fire from within the fort with shells with short fuses, thrown over the ridge by hand, like grenades, and these did some execution. The wounds inflicted by these missiles were frightful. To this we replied as actively as possible, and this conflict between parties invisible to each other, not only on account of the darkness, but also on account of the barrier between them, was kept up with fury during the night and the next forenoon. Immediately on the springing of the mine a tremendous cannonade was opened along our whole line, accompanied by active firing from the rifle-pits. This fire was continued with little relaxation during the night and the next day. After several days of this kind of warfare, we had made no progress whatever, not being able either to plant a battery or to open a rifle-pit upon the new ground.

Eventually McPherson completed another mine, which he exploded on the first day of July. Many Confederates were killed, and six were thrown over into our lines by the explosion. They were all dead but one, a negro, who got well and joined our army. McPherson did not, however, get possession of the place through this mine, as he had hoped.

Little advancement was made in the siege after McPherson sprang his first mine on the 25th of June, except in the matter of time and in the holding of the lines of investment. Several things conspired to produce inactivity and a sort of listlessness among the various commands—the heat of the weather, the unexpected length of the siege, the endurance of the defense, the absence of any thorough organization of the engineer department, and, above all, the well-grounded general belief of our officers and men that the town must presently fall through starvation, without any special effort or sacrifice. This belief was founded on the reports from within Vicksburg. Every new party of deserters which reached us agreed that the provisions of the place were near the point of total exhaustion, that rations had been reduced lower than ever, that extreme dissatisfaction existed among the garrison, and it was generally expected—indeed, there was a sort of conviction—on all hands that the city would be surrendered on Saturday, July 4th, if, indeed, it could hold out so long as that.

While apathy grew in our ranks, the Confederates displayed more activity than ever. On the morning of June 27th they sprang a countermine on Sherman's front, which destroyed the mines Sherman's engineers had nearly finished, and threw the head of his sap into general confusion. McPherson was prevented from taking possession of the fort, which had been partially destroyed. Ord's (lately McClernand's) working parties, which were now well up to the Confederate lines, were checked by hand grenades. Lauman was almost nightly assailed by little sorties of the enemy, and always lost a few men in them, killed, wounded, or captured.

The operations west of the Mississippi became more threatening, too. Our scouts brought in word that Price and Kirby Smith were about to attempt to provision Vicksburg by way of Milliken's Bend. There were rumors also that some two thousand or more skiffs had been prepared within the town, by which it was thought the garrison might escape.

The general indisposition of our troops to prosecute the siege zealously, and the evident determination on the part of the enemy to hold out until the last, caused General Grant to hold a council of war on the morning of June 30th, to take judgment on the question of trying another general assault, or leaving the result to the exhaustion of the garrison. The conclusion of the council was in favor of the latter policy, but two days later, July 2d, Grant told me that if the enemy did not give up Vicksburg by the 6th he should storm it.

Happily, there was no need to wait until the 6th. The general expectation that something would happen by July 4th was about to be confirmed. On the morning of Friday, July 3d, a soldier appeared on the Con- federate line, in McPherson's front, bearing a flag of truce. General A. J. Smith was sent to meet this man, who proved to be an officer, General J. S. Bowen. He bore a letter from Pemberton addressed to Grant. The letter was taken to headquarters, where it was read by the general and its contents were made known to the staff. It was a request for an armistice to arrange terms for the capitulation of Vicksburg. To this end Pemberton asked that three commissioners be appointed to meet a like number to be named by himself. Grant immediately wrote this reply:

> The useless effusion of blood you propose stopping by this course can be ended at any time you may choose by an unconditional surrender of the city and garrison. Men who have shown so much endurance and courage as those now in Vicksburg will always

challenge the respect of an adversary, and I can assure you will be treated with all the respect due to prisoners of war.

I do not favor the proposition of appointing commissioners to arrange terms of capitulation, because I have no terms other than those indicated above.

Bowen, the bearer of Pemberton's letter, who had been received by A. J. Smith, expressed a strong desire to converse with General Grant. While declining this, Grant requested Smith to say to Bowen that if General Pemberton desired to see him an interview would be granted between the lines in McPherson's front at any hour in the afternoon which Pemberton might appoint. After Bowen's departure a message was soon sent back to Smith, accepting the proposal for an interview, and appointing three o'clock as the hour.

Grant was there with his staff and with Generals Ord, McPherson, Logan, and A. J. Smith. Sherman was not present, being with his command watching Joe Johnston, and ready to spring upon the latter as soon as Pemberton was captured. Pemberton came late, attended by General Bowen and Colonel L. M. Montgomery.

It must have been a bitter moment for the Confederate chieftain. Pemberton was a Northern man, a Pennsylvanian by birth, from which State he was appointed to West Point, graduating in 1837. In the old army he fell under the spell of the influence of Jefferson Davis, whose close friend he was. Davis appears to have thought Pemberton was a military genius, for he was jumped almost at a stroke, without much previous service, to be a lieutenant general, and the defense of the Mississippi River was given over to his charge. His dispositions throughout the entire campaign, after Grant crossed at Bruinsburg, were weak, and he was easily overcome, although his troops fought well. As Joe Johnston truthfully remarks in his Narrative, Pemberton did not understand Grant's warfare at all. Penned up and finally compelled to surrender a vital post and a great army to his conqueror, an almost irremediable disaster to his cause, Pemberton not only suffered the usual pangs of defeat, but he was doubly humiliated by the knowledge that he would be suspected and accused of treachery by his adopted brethren, and that the result would be used by the enemies of Davis, whose favorite he was, to undermine the Confederate administration. As the events proved, it was indeed a great blow to Davis's hold upon the people of the South. These things must have passed through Pemberton's mind as he faced Grant for this final settlement of the fate of Vicksburg.

The conversation was held apart between Pemberton and his two officers and Grant, McPherson, and A. J. Smith, the rest of us being seated on the ground nearby.

We could, however, see that Pemberton was much excited, and was impatient in his answers to Grant. He insisted that his army be paroled and allowed to march beyond our lines, officers and all, with eight days' rations, drawn from their own stores, officers to retain their private property and body servants. Grant heard what Pemberton had to say, and left him at the end of an hour and a half, saying that he would send in his ultimatum in writing before evening; to this Pemberton promised to reply before night, hostilities to cease in the meantime. Grant then conferred at his headquarters with his corps and division commanders, all of whom, except Steele, who advised unconditional surrender, favored a plan proposed by McPherson, and finally adopted by Grant. The argument against the plan was one of feeling only. In its favor it was urged that it would at once not only tend to the demoralization of the enemy, but also release Grant's whole army for offensive operations against Joe Johnston and Port Hudson, while to guard and transport so many prisoners would require a great portion of our army's strength. Keeping the prisoners would also absorb all our steamboat transportation, while paroling them would leave it free to move our troops. Paroling would also save us an enormous expenditure.

After long consideration, General Grant reluctantly gave way to these reasons, and at six o'clock in the afternoon he sent a letter by the hands of General Logan and Lieutenant-Colonel Wilson, in which he stated as terms that, as soon as rolls could be made out and paroles signed by officers and men, Pemberton would be allowed to march out of our lines, the officers taking with them their side-arms and clothing, and the field, staff, and cavalry officers one horse each. The rank and file were to retain all their clothing, but no other property. If these conditions were accepted, any amount of rations deemed necessary was to be taken from the stores they had, besides the necessary cooking utensils. Thirty wagons also, counting two two-horse or mule teams as one, were to be allowed to transport such articles as could not be carried along. The same conditions were allowed to all sick and wounded officers and soldiers as fast as they became able to travel.

The officer who received this letter stated that it would be impossible to answer it by night, and it was not till a little before peep of day that the reply was furnished. In the main the terms were accepted, but Pemberton proposed as amendments:

> At 10 a. m. tomorrow I propose to evacuate the works in and around Vicksburg, and to surrender the city and garrison under my command by marching out with my colors and arms, stacking them in front of my present lines, after which you will take possession. Officers to retain their side-arms and personal property, and the rights and property of citizens to be respected.

General Grant immediately replied:

> I can make no stipulations with regard to the treatment of citizens and their private property. . . . The property which officers will be allowed to take with them will be as stated in my proposition of last evening. . . . If you mean by your proposition for each brigade to march to the front of the line now occupied by it, and stack arms at 10 A. M., and then return to the inside and there remain as prisoners until properly paroled, I will make no objection to it.
>
> Should no notification be received of your acceptance of my terms by 9 a. m., I shall regard them as having been rejected, and shall act accordingly.

The answer came back promptly, "The terms proposed by you are accepted."

Just the day before, General George Gordon Meade had consummated his great victory at Gettysburg.—Ed. 2018

We had a glorious celebration that day. Pemberton's note had been received just after daylight, and at the appointed hour of ten o'clock the surrender was consummated, the Confederate troops marching out and stacking arms in front of their works, while Pemberton appeared for a moment with his staff upon the parapet of the central fort. At eleven o'clock Grant entered the city. He was received by Pemberton with more marked impertinence than at their former interview. Grant bore it like a philosopher, and in reply treated Pemberton with even gentler courtesy and dignity than before.

I rode into Vicksburg at the side of the conqueror, and afterward perambulated among the conquered. The Confederate soldiers were generally more contented even than we were. Now they were going home, they said. They had had enough of the war. The cause of the Confederacy was lost. They wanted to take the oath of allegiance many of them. I was not surprised to learn a month later that of the twenty-odd thousand well men who were paroled at Vicksburg the greater part had since dispersed, and I felt sure they could never be got to serve again. The officers, on the other hand, all declared their determination never to give in. They had mostly on that day the look of men who have been crying all night. One major, who commanded a regiment from Missouri, burst into tears as he followed his disarmed men back into their lines after they had surrendered their colors and the guns in front of them.

I found the buildings of Vicksburg much less damaged than I had expected. Still, there were a good many people living in caves dug in the banks. Naturally the shells did less damage to these vaults than to dwellings. There was a considerable supply of railroad cars in the town, with one or two railroad locomotives in working condition. There was also an unexpected quantity of military supplies. At the end of the first week after our entrance sixty-six thousand stand of small arms had been collected, mainly in good condition, and more were constantly being discovered. They were concealed in caves, as well as in all sorts of buildings. The siege and seacoast guns found exceeded sixty, and the whole captured artillery was above two hundred pieces. The stores of rebel ammunition also proved to be surprisingly heavy. As Grant expressed it, there was enough to have kept up the defense for six years at the rate they were using it. The stock of army clothing was officially invoiced at five million dollars—Confederate prices. Of sugar, molasses, and salt there was a large quantity, and sixty thousand pounds of bacon were found in one place.

The way in which Grant handled his army at the capitulation of Vicksburg was a splendid example of his energy. As soon as negotiations for surrender began on the 3d, he sent word to Sherman, at his camp on Bear Creek, to get ready to move against Johnston. Sherman always acted on the instant, and that very afternoon he threw bridges across the Big Black. He started his forces over the river on the 4th as soon as he received word that Pemberton had accepted Grant's ultimatum.

In the meantime Grant had ordered part of Ord's corps, all of Steele's division, and the two divisions of the Ninth Corps, which was at Haynes's Bluff, to be ready to join Sherman as soon as the capitulation was effected. Their movement was so prompt that by Sunday night, July 5th, part of Ord's force was across the Big Black and Steele was well up to the river.

As Grant supposed that Banks needed help at Port Hudson, he had sent a messenger to him on the 1st of the month telling him the surrender was imminent, and offering aid if he needed it. A division—that of Herron—was now made ready to march as soon as word came back. In the city itself there was the greatest activity. The occupation of the place by our forces was directed by General McPherson, who was appointed to the command. Three divisions were detailed to garrison the line of fortifications and to furnish the guards for the interior of the city. By the night of the 5th no troops remained outside of Vicksburg.

The paroling of the Confederate troops began as soon as the occupation was complete, and was pushed with all possible rapidity. At the same time those parts of the fortifications which we were now to defend were selected, and the men began to obliterate the siege approaches at which they had worked so hard and so long. So busy was Grant with the mobilization of his army for offensive field operations and the garrisoning of Vicksburg that he did not take time even to write to Washington. My telegram of July 5th to Mr. Stanton describing the surrender and the condition of things in Vicksburg conveyed this request from Grant for instructions from Washington:

> General Grant, being himself intensely occupied, desires me to say that he would like to receive from General Halleck as soon as practicable either general or specific instructions as to the future conduct of the war in his department. He has no idea of going into summer quarters, nor does he doubt his ability to employ his army so as to make its blows tell toward the great result; but he would like to be informed whether the Government wishes him to follow his own judgment or to co-operate in some particular scheme of operations.

With the fall of Vicksburg my mission was at an end. On the 6th of July I left Grant for the North, stopping at Helena, Ark., on my way up the river long enough to get news of Gen. Prentiss's recent operations. Thence I went on to Cairo and Washington.

WITH THE ARMY OF THE CUMBERLAND

I happened to be the first man to reach the capital from Vicksburg, and everybody wanted to hear the story and to ask questions. I was anxious to get home and see my family, however, and left for New York as soon as I could get away. A few days after I arrived in New York I received an invitation to go into business there with Mr. Ketchum, a banker, and with George Opdyke, the merchant. I wrote Mr. Stanton of the opening, but he urged me to remain in the War Department as one of his assistants, which I consented to do.

Although appointed some months before, Mr. Dana was not nominated in the Senate as Second Assistant Secretary of War until January 20, 1864; the nomination was confirmed on January 26.—note in original

The first commission with which Mr. Stanton charged me after my appointment as his assistant was one similar to that which I had just finished—to go to Tennessee to observe and report the movements of Rosecrans against Bragg. General Rosecrans, who, after the battle of Stone's River, or Murfreesboro, on December 31st to January 2, 1863, had lain for nearly six months at Murfreesboro, obstructing on various excuses all the efforts Lincoln and Stanton and Halleck put forth to make him move against Bragg, who occupied what was known as the Tullahoma line, had toward the end of June moved on Bragg and driven him across the Tennessee River. He had then settled down to rest again, while Bragg had taken possession of his new line in and about Chattanooga.

Burnside, who was in Kentucky, had been ordered to unite with Rosecrans by way of East Tennessee, in order that the combined force should attack Bragg, but, despite the urgency of the administration, no movement was made by Rosecrans until the middle of August. As soon as it was evident that he was really going out against the Confederates, Mr. Stanton asked me to join the Army of the Cumberland. My orders were to report directly to

Rosecrans's headquarters. I carried the following letter of introduction to that general:

> War Department, Washington City,
>
> August 30, 1863.
>
> Maj.-Gen. Rosecrans, Commanding, etc.
>
> General : This will introduce to you Charles A. Dana, Esq., one of my assistants, who visits your command for the purpose of conferring with you upon any subject which you may desire to have brought to the notice of the department. Mr. Dana is a gentleman of distinguished character, patriotism, and ability, and possesses the entire confidence of the department. You will please afford to him the courtesy and consideration which he merits, and explain to him fully any matters which you may desire through him to bring to the notice of the department.
>
> Yours truly,
>
> Edwin M. Stanton.

As soon as my papers arrived I left for my post. I was much delayed on railroads and steamboats, and when I reached Cincinnati found it was impossible to join Burnside by his line of march to Knoxville and from him go to Rosecrans, as I had intended. Accordingly I went on to Louisville, where I arrived on September 5th. I found there that Burnside had just occupied Knoxville; that the Ninth Corps, which two months before I had left near Vicksburg, was now about to go to him from near Louisville; and that Rosecrans had queerly enough telegraphed to the clergy all over the country that he expected a great battle that day and desired their prayers.

I went directly from Louisville to Nashville, where I found General Gordon Granger in command. As he and Governor Johnson were going to the front in a day or two, I waited to go with them. The morning after my arrival at Nashville I went to call on Johnson. I had never met him before.

Andrew Johnson [Lincoln's successor as president] was short and stocky, of dark complexion, smooth face, dark hair, dark eyes, and of great determination of appearance. When I went to see him in his office, the first thing he said was:

"Will you have a drink?"

"Yes, I will," I answered. So he brought out a jug of whisky and poured out as much as he wanted in a tumbler, and then made it about half and half water. The theoretical, philosophical drinker pours out a little whisky and puts in almost no water at all—drinks it pretty nearly pure—but when a man gets to taking a good deal of water in his whisky, it shows he is in the habit of drinking a good deal. I noticed that the Governor took more whisky than most gentlemen would have done, and I concluded that he took it pretty often.

I had a prolonged conversation that morning with Governor Johnson, who expressed himself in cheering terms in regard to the general condition of Tennessee. He regarded the occupation of Knoxville by Burnside as completing the permanent expulsion of Confederate power, and said he should order a general election for the first week in October. He declared that slavery was destroyed in fact, but must be abolished legally. Johnson was thoroughly in favor of immediate emancipation both as a matter of moral right and as an indispensable condition of the large immigration of industrious freemen which he thought necessary to repeople and regenerate the State.

On the 10th of September we started for the front, going by rail to Bridgeport, on the Tennessee River. This town at that date was the terminus of the Nashville and Chattanooga Railroad. The bridge across the river and part of the railroad beyond had been destroyed by Bragg when he retreated in the preceding summer from Tullahoma. It was by way of Bridgeport that troops were joining Rosecrans at the far front, and all supplies went to him that way. On reaching the town,

106 we heard that Chattanooga had been occupied by Crittenden's corps of Rosecrans's army the day before, September 9th; so the next day, September 11th, I pushed on there by horseback past Shellmound and Wauhatchie. The country

through which I passed is a magnificent region of rocks and valleys, and I don't believe there is anywhere a finer view than that I had from Lookout Mountain as I approached Chattanooga.

When I reached Chattanooga I went at once to General Rosecrans's headquarters and presented my letter. He read it, and then burst out in angry abuse of the Government at Washington. He had not been sustained, he said. His requests had been ignored, his plans thwarted. Both Stanton and Halleck had done all they could, he declared, to prevent his success.

"General Rosecrans," I said, "I have no authority to listen to complaints against the Government. I was sent here for the purpose of finding out what the Government could do to aid you, and have no right to confer with you on other matters."

He quieted down at once, and explained his situation to me. He had reached Chattanooga, he said, on the 10th, with Crittenden's troops, the Twenty-first Corps, the town having been evacuated the day before by the Confederates. As all the reports brought in seemed to indicate that Bragg was in full retreat toward Rome, Ga., Crittenden had immediately started in pursuit, and had gone as far as Ringgold. On the night before (September 11th) it had seemed evident that Bragg had abandoned his retreat on Rome, and behind the curtain of the woods and hills had returned with the purpose of suddenly falling with his whole army upon the different corps and divisions of our army, now widely separated by the necessity of crossing the mountains at gaps far apart.

General Thomas Leonidas Crittenden (1819 – 1893) was a lawyer and politician. On June 25, 1876, his son Lieutenant John Crittenden died with Custer at the Battle of the Little Bighorn. When Phil Sheridan's brother, Michael, was sent in 1877 to recover the remains of 7th Cavalry officers, Crittenden was the only parent of Custer's fallen officers to direct that his son's remains be left buried where he fell.—Ed. 2018

This was a serious matter for Rosecrans, if true, for at that moment his army was scattered over a line more than fifty miles long, extending from Chattanooga on the north to Alpine on the south. Rosecrans pointed out to me the positions on the map.

Crittenden, he explained, had been ordered immediately to leave Ring-gold and move westward to the valley of the West Chickamauga. He was near a place known as Lee and Gordon's Mills. General Thomas, who commanded the Fourteenth Corps, had marched across Lookout Mountain and now held Stevens's Gap, perhaps twenty-five miles south of Chattanooga. McCook, with the Twentieth Corps, had been ordered, after crossing the Tennessee, to march southeast, and now was at Alpine, fully thirty-five miles south of Crittenden. Orders had been sent McCook, when it was found that Bragg had made a stand, to rest his left flank on the southern base of Mission Ridge, and, extending his line toward Summerville, fall on the flank of the enemy should he follow the valley that way. The reserve, under Gordon Granger, was still north of the Tennessee, although one division had reached Bridgeport and the rest were rapidly approaching. Notwithstanding the signs that Bragg might not be retreating so fast as he at first appeared to have been, Rosecrans was confident as late as the 12th that the Confederate commander was merely making a show of the offensive to check pursuit, and that he would make his escape to Rome as soon as he found our army concentrated for battle east of Lookout Mountain.

The next day (the 13th) I left Chattanooga with Rosecrans and his staff for Thomas's headquarters at Stevens's Gap. We found everything progressing favorably there. The movements for the concentration of the three corps were going forward with energy. Scouts were coming in constantly, who reported that the enemy had withdrawn from the basin where our army was assembling; that he was evacuating Lafayette and moving toward Rome. It seemed as if at last the Army of the Cumberland had practically gained a position from which it could effectually advance upon Rome and Atlanta, and deliver there the finishing blow of the war. The difficulties of gaining this position, of crossing the Cumberland Mountains, passing the Tennessee, turning and occupying Chattanooga, traversing the mountain ridges of northern Georgia, and seizing the passes which led southward had been enormous. It was only when I came personally to examine the region that I appreciated what had been done. These difficulties were all substantially overcome. The army was in the best possible condition, and was advancing with all the rapidity which the nature of the country allowed. Our left flank toward East Tennessee was secured by Burnside, and the only disadvantage which I could see was that a sudden movement of the enemy to our right might endanger our long and precarious line of communications and compel us to retreat again beyond the Tennessee. I felt this so keenly that I urged Mr. Stanton, in a dispatch sent to him on the 14th from Thomas's headquarters, to push as strong a column as possible eastward from Corinth, in northeastern Mississippi. It seemed to me that it would be better to recall the troops from the West rather than to risk a check here, where the heart of rebellion was within reach and the final blow all prepared.

But, after all, there was something of a mystery about the real location of Bragg's army, its strength, and the designs of its chief. At any rate it was soon manifest that Bragg was not withdrawing to the southward, as at first supposed. Some queer developments down the Chickamauga on the 16th and 17th caused Rosecrans considerable anxiety for Chattanooga. The impression began to grow, too, that Bragg had been playing 'possum, and had not retreated at all. Rosecrans at once abandoned all idea of operations against the Confederate line of retreat and supply, drew his army in rapidly, and began to look sharply after his own communications with Chattanooga, which had now become his base.

By noon of September 18th the concentration was practically complete. Our army then lay up and down the valley, with West Chickamauga Creek in front of the greater part of the line. The left was held by Crittenden, the center by Thomas, and the right by McCook, whose troops were now all in the valley except one brigade. The army had not concentrated any too soon, for that very afternoon the enemy appeared on our left, and a considerable engagement occurred. It was said at headquarters that a battle was certain the no next day. The only point Rosecrans had not determined at five o'clock on the afternoon of the 18th was whether to make a night march and fall on Bragg at daylight or to await his onset.

But that night it became pretty clear to all that Bragg's plan was to push by our left into Chattanooga. This compelled another rapid movement by the left down the Chickamauga. By a tiresome night march Thomas moved down behind Crittenden and below Lee and Gordon's Mills, taking position on our extreme left. Crittenden followed, connecting with Thomas's right, and thus taking position in the center. McCook's corps also extended downstream to the left, but still covered the creek as high up as Crawfish Spring, while part of his troops acted as a reserve. These movements were hurriedly made, and the troops, especially those of Thomas, were very much exhausted by their efforts to get into position.

Rosecrans had not been mistaken in Bragg's intention. About nine o'clock the next morning at Crawfish Spring, where the general headquarters were, we heard firing on our left, and reports at once came in that the battle had begun there, Bragg being in command of the enemy. Thomas had barely headed the Confederates off from Chattanooga. We remained at Crawfish Springs on this day until after one o'clock, waiting for the full proportions of the conflict to develop. When it became evident that the battle was being fought entirely on our left, Rosecrans removed his headquarters nearer to the scene, taking a little house near Lee and Gordon's Mills, known as the Widow Glenn's. Although closer to the battle, we could see no more of it here than at Crawfish Springs, the conflict being fought altogether in a thick forest, and being invisible to outsiders. The nature of the firing and the reports from the commanders alone enabled us to follow its progress.

That we were able to keep as well informed as we were was due to our excellent telegraphic communications. By this time the military telegraph had been so thoroughly developed that it was one of the most useful accessories of our army, even on a battlefield. For instance, after Rosecrans had taken Crawfish Springs as his headquarters, he had given orders, on September

17th, to connect the place with Chattanooga, thirteen miles to the northwest. The line was completed after the battle began on the 19th, and we were in communication not only with Chattanooga, but with Granger at Rossville and with Thomas at his headquarters. When Rosecrans removed to the Widow Glenn's, the telegraphers went along, and in an hour had connections made and an instrument clicking away in Mrs. Glenn's house. We thus had constant information of the way the battle was going, not only from the orderlies, but also from the wires.

This excellent arrangement enabled me also to keep the Government at Washington informed of the progress of the battle. I sent eleven dispatches that day to Mr. Stanton. They were very brief, but they reported all that I, near as I was to the scene, knew of the battle of September 19th at Chickamauga.

It was not till after dark that firing ceased and final reports began to come in. From these we found that the enemy had been defeated in his attempt to turn and crush our left flank and secure possession of the Chattanooga roads, but that he was not wholly defeated, for he still held his ground in several places, and was preparing, it was believed, to renew the battle the next day.

That evening Rosecrans decided that if Bragg did not retreat he would renew the fight at daylight, and a council of war was held at our headquarters at the Widow Glenn's, to which all the corps and division commanders were summoned. There must have been ten or twelve general officers there. Rosecrans began by asking each of the corps commanders for a report of the condition of his troops and of the position they occupied; also for his opinion of what was to be done. Each proposition was discussed by the entire council as it was made. General Thomas was so tired—he had not slept at all the night before, and he had been in battle all day—that he went to sleep every minute. Every time Rosecrans spoke to him he would straighten up and answer, but he always said the same thing, "I would strengthen the left," and then he would be asleep, sitting up in his chair. General Rosecrans, to the proposition to strengthen the left, made always the same reply, "Where are we going to take it from?"

After the discussion was ended, Rosecrans gave his orders for the disposition of the troops on the following day. Thomas's corps was to remain on the left with his line somewhat drawn in, but substantially as he was at the close of the day. McCook was to close on Thomas and cover the position at Widow Glenn's, and Crittenden was to have two divisions in reserve near the junction of McCook's and Thomas's lines, to be able to succor either. These orders were written for each corps commander. They were also read in the presence of all, and the plans fully explained. Finally, after everything had been said, hot coffee was brought in, and then McCook was called upon to sing the Hebrew Maiden. McCook sang the song, and then the council broke up and the generals went away.

This was about midnight, and, as I was very tired, I lay down on the floor to sleep, beside Captain Horace Porter,* who was at that time Rosecrans's chief of ordnance. There were cracks in the floor of the Widow Glenn's house, and the wind blew up under us. We would go to sleep, and then the wind would come up so cold through the cracks that it would wake us up, and we would turn over together to keep warm.

Horace Porter wrote one of the most interesting memoirs of time spent with Grant in the war. Porter wanted an active command of his own but Grant felt he could not spare him from the staff. He later served in Grant's presidential administration. See Campaigning with Grant.—Ed. 2018

At daybreak we at headquarters were all up and on our horses ready to go with the commanding general to inspect our lines. We rode past McCook, Crittenden, and Thomas to the extreme left, Rosecrans giving as he went the orders he thought necessary to strengthen the several positions. The general intention of these orders was to close up on the left, where it was evident the attack would begin. We then rode back to the extreme right, Rosecrans stopping at each point to see if his orders had been obeyed. In several cases they had not been obeyed, and he made them more peremptory. When we found that McCook's line had been elongated so that it was a mere thread, Rosecrans was very angry, and sent for the general, rebuking him severely, although, as a matter of fact, General McCook's position had been taken under the written orders of the commander in chief, given the night before.

About half past eight or nine o'clock the battle began on the left, where Thomas was. At that time Rosecrans, with whom I always remained, was on the right, directing the movements of the troops there. Just after the cannon began I remember that a ten-pound shell came crashing through our staff, but hurting nobody. I had not slept much for two nights, and, as it was warm, I dismounted about noon and, giving my horse to my orderly, lay down on the grass and went to sleep. I was awakened by the most infernal noise I ever heard. Never in any battle I had witnessed was there such a discharge of cannon and musketry. I sat up on the grass, and the first thing I saw was General Rosecrans crossing himself—he was a very devout Catholic. "Hello!" I said to myself, "if the general is crossing himself, we are in a desperate situation."

I was on my horse in a moment. I had no sooner collected my thoughts and looked around toward the front, where all this din came from, than I saw our lines break and melt away like leaves before the wind. Then the headquarters around me disappeared. The gray-backs came through with a rush, and soon the musket balls and the cannon shot began to reach the place where we stood. The whole right of the army had apparently been routed. My orderly stuck to me like a veteran, and we drew back for greater safety into the woods a little way. There I came upon General Porter—Captain Porter he was then—and Captain Drouillard, an aide-de-camp infantry officer attached to General Rosecrans's staff, halting fugitives. They would halt a few of them, get them into some sort of a line, and make a beginning of order among them, and then there would come a few rounds of cannon shot through the tree-tops over their heads and the men would break and run. I saw Porter and Drouillard plant themselves in front of a body of these stampeding men and command them to halt. One man charged with his bayonet, menacing Porter; but

Porter held his ground, and the man gave in. That was the only case of real mutiny that I ever saw in the army, and that was under such circumstances that the man was excusable. The cause of all this disaster was the charge of the Confederates through the hiatus in the line caused by the withdrawal of Wood's division, under a misapprehension of orders, before its place could be filled.

I attempted to make my way from this point in the woods to Sheridan's division, but when I reached the place where I knew it had been a little time before, I found it had been swept from the field. Not far away, however, I stumbled on a body of organized troops. This was a brigade of mounted riflemen under Colonel John T. Wilder, of Indiana. "Mr. Dana," asked Colonel Wilder, "what is the situation?"

"I do not know," I said, "except that this end of the army has been routed. There is still heavy fighting at the left front, and our troops seem to be holding their ground there yet."

"Will you give me any orders?" he asked.

"I have no authority to give orders" I replied; "but if I were in your situation I should go to the left, where Thomas is."

Then I turned my horse, and, making my way over Missionary Ridge, struck the Chattanooga Valley and rode to Chattanooga, twelve or fifteen miles away. The whole road was filled with flying soldiers; here and there were pieces of artillery, caissons, and baggage wagons. Everything was in the greatest disorder. When I reached Chattanooga, a little before four o'clock, I found Rosecrans there. In the helter-skelter to the rear he had escaped by the Rossville road. He was expecting every moment that the enemy would arrive before the town, and was doing all he could to prepare to resist his entrance. Soon after I arrived the two corps commanders, McCook and Crittenden, both came into Chattanooga.

The first thing I did on reaching town was to telegraph Mr. Stanton. I had not sent him any telegrams in the morning, for I had been in the field with Rosecrans, and part of the time at some distance from the Widow Glenn's, where the operators were at work. The boys kept at their post there until the Confederates swept them out of the house. When they had to run, they went instruments and tools in hand, and as soon as out of reach of the enemy set up shop on a stump. It was not long before they were driven out of this. They next attempted to establish an office on the Rossville road, but before they had succeeded in making connections a battle was raging around them, and they had to retreat to Granger's headquarters at Rossville.

Having been swept bodily off the battlefield, and having made my way into Chattanooga through a panic-stricken rabble, the first telegram which I sent to Mr. Stanton was naturally colored by what I had seen and experienced. I remember that I began the dispatch by saying: "My report today is of deplorable importance. Chickamauga is as fatal a name in our history as Bull Run." By eight o'clock that evening, however, I found that I had given too dark a view of the disaster.

Early the next morning things looked still better. Rosecrans received a telegram from Thomas at Rossville, to which point he had withdrawn after the nightfall, saying that his troops were in high spirits, and that he had brought off all his wounded. A little while before noon General [and future president] James A. Garfield, who was chief of Rosecrans's staff, arrived in Chattanooga and gave us the first connected account we had of the battle on the left after the rout. Garfield said that he had become separated from Rosecrans in the rout of our right wing and had made his way to the left, and spent the afternoon and night with General Thomas. There he witnessed the sequel of the battle in that part of the field. Thomas, finding himself cut off from Rosecrans and the right, at once marshalled the remaining divisions for independent fighting. Refusing both his right and left, his line assumed the form of a horseshoe, posted along the slope and crest of a partly wooded ridge. He was soon joined by Granger from Rossville, with Steedman and most of the reserve; and with these forces, more than two thirds of the army, he firmly maintained the fight till after dark. Our troops were as immovable as the rocks they stood on. Longstreet hurled against them repeatedly the dense columns which had routed Davis and Sheridan in the early afternoon, but every onset was repulsed with dreadful slaughter. Falling first on one and then another point of our lines, for hours the rebels vainly sought to break them. Thomas seemed to have filled every soldier with his own unconquerable firmness, and Granger, his hat torn by bullets, raged like a lion wherever the combat was hottest with the electrical courage of a Ney. When night fell, this body of heroes stood on the same ground they had occupied in the morning, their spirit unbroken, but their numbers greatly diminished.

THE REMOVAL OF ROSECRANS

All the news we could get the next day of the enemy's movements seemed to show that the Confederate forces were concentrating on Chattanooga. Accordingly, Rosecrans gave orders for all our troops to gather in the town at once and prepare for the attack which would probably take place within a day or two. By midnight the army was in Chattanooga. The troops were in wonderful spirits, considering their excessive fatigues and heavy losses, and the next morning went to work with energy on the fortifications. All the morning of the 22d the enemy were approaching, resisted by our advance parties, and by the middle of the afternoon the artillery firing was so near that it seemed certain that the battle would be fought before dark. No attack was made that day, however, nor the next, and by the morning of the 24th the Herculean labors of the army had so fortified the place that it was certain that it could be taken only by a regular siege or by a turning movement. The strength of our forces was about forty-five thousand effective men, and we had ten days' full rations on hand. Chattanooga could hold out, but it was apparent that no offensive operations were possible until re-enforcements came. These we knew had been hurried toward us as soon as the news of the disaster of the 20th reached Washington. Burnside was coming from Knoxville, we supposed, Hooker had been ordered from Washington by rail, Sherman from Vicksburg by steamer, and some of Hurlbut's troops from Memphis.

The enemy by the 24th were massed in Chattanooga Valley, and held Missionary Ridge and Lookout Mountain. The summit of Lookout Mountain, almost the key to Chattanooga, was not given up by Rosecrans until the morning of the 24th; then he ordered the withdrawal of the brigade which held the heights, and the destruction of the wagon road which winds along its side at about one third of its height and connects the valleys of Chattanooga and Lookout. Both Granger and Garfield earnestly protested against this order, contending that the mountain and the road could be held by not more than seven regiments against the whole power of the enemy. They were obviously right, but Rosecrans was sometimes as obstinate and inaccessible to reason as at others he was irresolute, vacillating, and inconclusive, and he pettishly rejected all their arguments. The mountain was given up.

As soon as we felt reasonably sure that Chattanooga could hold out until re-enforcements came, the disaster of the 20th of September became the absorbing topic of conversation in the Army of the Cumberland. At headquarters, in camp, in the street, on the fortifications, officers and soldiers and citizens wrangled over the reasons for the loss of the day. By the end of the first week after the disaster a serious fermentation reigned in the Twentieth and Twenty-first Army Corps, and, indeed, throughout the whole army, growing out of events connected with the battle.

There was at once a manifest disposition to hold McCook and Crittenden, the commanders of the two corps, responsible, because they had left the field of battle amid the rout of the right wing and made their way to Chattanooga.

The feeling of the army toward McCook and Crittenden was afterward greatly modified. A court of inquiry examined their cases, and in February, 1864, gave its final finding and opinion. McCook it relieved entirely from responsibility for the reverse of September 20th, declaring that the small force at his disposal was inadequate to defend, against greatly superior numbers, the long line he had taken under instructions, and adding that, after the line was broken, he had done everything he could to rally and hold his troops, giving the necessary orders to his subordinates. General Crittenden's conduct, the court likewise declared, showed no cause for censure, and he was in no way responsible for the disaster to the right wing.—note in original

It was not generally understood or appreciated at that time that, because of Thomas's repeated calls for aid and Rosecrans's consequent alarm for his left, Crittenden had been stripped of all his troops and had no infantry whatever left to command, and that McCook's lines also had been reduced to a fragment by similar orders from Rosecrans and by fighting. A strong opposition to both sprang up, which my telegrams to Mr. Stanton immediately after the battle fully reflect. The generals of division and of brigade felt the situation deeply, and said that they could no longer serve under such superiors, and that, if this was required of them, they must resign. This feeling was universal among them, including men like Major-Generals Palmer and Sheridan and Brigadier-Generals Wood, Johnson, and Hazen.

The feeling of these officers did not seem in the least to partake of a mutinous or disorderly character; it was rather conscientious unwillingness to risk their men and the country's cause in hands which they thought to be unsafe. No formal representation of this unwillingness was made to Rosecrans, but he was made aware of the state of things by private conversations with several of the parties. The defects of his character complicated the difficulty. He abounded in friendliness and approbativeness [sic], and was greatly lacking in firmness and steadiness of will. In short, he was a temporizing man; he dreaded so heavy an alternative as was now presented, and hated to break with McCook and Crittenden.

Besides, there was a more serious obstacle to Rosecrans's acting decisively in the fact that if Crittenden and McCook had gone to Chattanooga, with the sound of artillery in their ears, from that glorious field where Thomas and Granger were saving their army and their country's honor, he had gone to Chattanooga also. It might be said in his excuse that, under the circumstances of the sudden rout, it was perfectly proper for the commanding general to go to the rear to prepare the next line of defense. Still, Rosecrans felt that that excuse could not entirely clear him either in his own eyes or in those of the army. In fact, it was perfectly plain that, while the subordinate commanders would not resign if he was retained in the chief command, as I believe they certainly would have done if McCook and Crittenden had not been relieved, their respect for Rosecrans as a general had received an irreparable blow.

The dissatisfaction with Rosecrans seemed to me to put the army into a very dangerous condition, and, in writing to Mr. Stanton on September 27th, I said that if it was decided to change the chief commander I would suggest that some Western commander of high rank and great prestige, like Grant, would be preferable as Rosecrans's successor to one who had hitherto commanded in the East alone.

The army, however, had its own candidate for Rosecrans's post. General Thomas had risen to the highest point in their esteem, as he had in that of everyone who witnessed his conduct on that unfortunate and glorious day, and I saw that, should there be a change in the chief command, there was no other man whose appointment would be so welcome. I earnestly recommended Mr. Stanton that in event of a change in the chief command Thomas's merits be considered. He was certainly an officer of the very highest qualities, soldierly and personally. He was a man of the greatest dignity of character. He had more the character of George Washington than any other man I ever knew. At the same time he was a delightful man to be with; there was no artificial dignity about Thomas. He was a West Point graduate, and very well educated. He was very set in his opinions, yet he was not impatient with anybody—a noble character.

In reply to my recommendation of Thomas, I received a telegram from the Secretary of War, saying: "I wish you to go directly to see General Thomas, and say to him that his services, his abilities, his character, his unselfishness, have always been most cordially appreciated by me, and that it is not my fault that he has not long since had command of an independent army." Accordingly, I went at once over to General Thomas's headquarters. I remember that I got there just after they had finished dinner; the table was not cleared off, but there was nobody in the dining room. When General Thomas came in, I read to him the telegram from the Secretary. He was too much affected by it to reply immediately. After a moment he said:

"Mr. Dana, I wish you would say to the Secretary of War that I am greatly affected by this expression of his confidence; that I should have long since liked to have had an independent command, but what I should have desired would have been the command of an army that I could myself have organized, disciplined, distributed, and combined. I wish you would add also that I would not like to take the command of an army where I should be exposed to the imputation of having intrigued or of having exercised any effort to supplant my previous commander."

This was on October 4th. Four days later General Thomas sent a confidential friend to me, saying rumors had come to him that he was to be put in Rosecrans's place; that, while he would gladly accept any other command to which Mr. Stanton should see fit to assign him, he could not consent to become the successor of General Rosecrans. He would not do anything to give countenance to the suspicion that he had intrigued against his commander's interest. He declared that he had perfect confidence in the fidelity and capacity of General Rosecrans.

The first change in the Army of the Cumberland was an order from Washington consolidating the Twentieth and Twenty-first Corps. The news reached Chattanooga on October 5th in a Nashville newspaper, and, not having been previously promulgated, it caused a sensation. Crittenden was much excited, and said that, as the Government no longer required his services, he would resign; at any rate, he would not hibernate like others, drawing pay and doing no work. McCook took it easily. The consolidation of the two corps was generally well received, and, as it was to be followed by a general reorganization of the army, it seemed as if the most happy consequences would be produced. The only serious difficulty which followed the change was that the men in the consolidated corps were troubled by letters from home, showing that their friends regarded a consolidation as a token of disgrace and punishment.

Although the reorganization of the army was going on, there was no real change in our situation, and by the middle of October it began to look as if we were in a helpless and precarious position. No re-enforcements had yet reached us, the enemy was growing stronger every day, and, worse still, we were threatened with starvation. Rosecrans's error in abandoning Lookout Mountain to the enemy on September 24th was now apparent. Our supplies came by rail from Nashville to Bridgeport; but the enemy controlled the south shore of the Tennessee between us and Bridgeport, and thus prevented our rebuilding the railroad from Bridgeport to Chattanooga; with their shore batteries they stopped the use of our steamboats. They even made the road on the north shore impassable, the sharpshooters on the south bank being able to pick off our men on the north. The forage and supplies which we had drawn from the country within our reach were now exhausted, and we were dependent upon what could be got to us over the roads north of the river. These were not only disturbed by the enemy, but were so bad in places that the mud was up to the horses' bellies. The animals themselves had become too weak to haul the empty train up the mountain, while many had died of starvation. On October 15th the troops were on half rations, and officers as they went about where the men were working on the fortifications frequently heard the cry of "Crackers!"

In the midst of these difficulties General Rosecrans seemed to be insensible to the impending danger; he dawdled with trifles in a manner which scarcely can be imagined. With plenty of zealous and energetic officers ready to do whatever needed to be done, precious time was lost because our dazed and mazy commander could not perceive the catastrophe that was close upon us, nor fix his mind upon the means of preventing it. I never saw anything which seemed so lamentable and hopeless. Our animals were starving, the men had starvation before them, and the enemy was bound soon to make desperate efforts to dislodge us. Yet the commanding general devoted that part of the time which was not employed in pleasant gossip to the composition of a long report to prove that the Government was to blame for his failure on the 20th.

While few persons exhibited more estimable social qualities, I have never seen a public man possessing talent with less administrative power, less clearness and steadiness in difficulty, and greater practical incapacity than General Rosecrans. He had inventive fertility and knowledge, but he had no strength of will and no concentration of purpose. His mind scattered; there was no system in the use of his busy days and restless nights, no courage against individuals in his composition, and, with great love of command, he was a feeble commander. He was conscientious and honest, just as he was imperious and disputatious; always with a stray vein of caprice and an overweening passion for the approbation of his personal friends and the public outside.

Although the army had been reorganized as a result of the consolidation of the Twentieth and Twenty-first Corps, it was still inefficient and its discipline defective. The former condition proceeded from the fact that General Rosecrans insisted on directing personally every department, and kept every one waiting and uncertain till he himself could directly supervise every operation. The latter proceeded from his utter lack of firmness, his passion for universal applause, and his incapacity to hurt any man's feelings by just severity.

My opinion of Rosecrans and my fears that the army would soon be driven from Chattanooga by starvation, if not by the Confederates, I had reiterated in my letters to Mr. Stanton. On the morning of October 19th I received a dispatch from Mr. Stanton, sent from Washington on October 16th, asking me to meet him that day at the Galt House in Louisville. I wired him that, unless he ordered to the contrary, Rosecrans would retreat at once from Chattanooga, and then I started for Louisville. It was a hard trip by horseback over Walden's Ridge and through Jasper to Bridgeport, and the roads were not altogether safe. Ten days before this, in riding along the edge of a bank near the river shore, the earth had given way under my horse's hind feet, and he and I had been tumbled together down a bank, about fourteen feet high; we rolled over each other in the sand at the bottom. I got off with no worse injury than a bruise of my left shoulder and a slight crack on the back of my head from the horse's hind foot, which made the blood run a little. The roads over Walden Ridge and along the river were even worse now than when I got my tumble, and, besides, they were filled with wagons trying to get supplies to Chattanooga. It took at that time ten days for wagon teams to go from Stevenson, where we had a depot, to Chattanooga. Though subsistence stores were so nearly exhausted, the wagons were compelled to throw overboard portions of their precious cargo in order to get through. The returning trains were blockaded. On the 17th of October five hundred teams were halted between the mountain and the river without forage for the animals, and unable to move in any direction; the whole road was strewn with dead animals.

The railway from Bridgeport to Nashville was not much more comfortable or safer than the road. Early in the month I had gone to Nashville on business, and had come back in a tremendous storm in a train of eighteen cars crowded with soldiers, and was twenty-six hours on the road instead of ten. On the present trip, however, I got along very well until within about eight miles from Nashville, when our train narrowly escaped destruction. A tie had been inserted in a cattle guard to throw the train down an embankment, but it had been calculated for a train going south, so that ours simply broke it off. From what we learned afterward, we thought it was intended for a train on which it was supposed General Grant was going to Bridgeport.

My train was bound through to Louisville. Indeed, I think there was no one with me except the train hands and the engineer. We reached Nashville about ten o'clock on the night of October 20th, and there were halted. Directly there came in an officer—I think it was Lieutenant-Colonel [Theodore] Bowers, of General Grant's staff—who said:

"General Grant wants to see you."

This was the first that I knew Grant was in Tennessee. I got out of my train and went over to his. I hadn't seen him since we parted at Vicksburg.

"I am going to interfere with your journey, Mr. Dana," he said as soon as I came in. "I have got the Secretary's permission to take you back with me to Chattanooga. I want you to dismiss your train and get in mine; we will give you comfortable quarters."

"General," I said, "did you ask the Secretary to let me go back with you?"

"I did," he said; "I wanted to have you."

So, of course, I went. On the way down he told me that he had been appointed to the command of the "Military Division of the Mississippi," with permission to leave Rosecrans in command of the Department of the Cumberland or to assign Thomas in his place. He had done the latter, he said, and had telegraphed Thomas to take charge of the army the night after Stanton, at Louisville, had received my dispatch of the 19th saying Rosecrans would retreat from Chattanooga unless ordered to remain. Rosecrans was assigned to the Department of the Missouri, with headquarters at St. Louis.

CHATTANOOGA AND MISSIONARY RIDGE

With Grant I left Nashville for the front on the morning of the 21st. We arrived safe in Bridgeport in the evening. The next morning, October 22d, we left on horseback for Chattanooga by way of Jasper and Walden's Ridge. The roads were in such a condition that it was impossible for Grant, who was on crutches from an injury to his leg received by the fall of a horse in New Orleans some time before, to make the whole distance of fifty-five miles in one day, so I pushed on ahead, running the rebel picket lines, and reaching Chattanooga in the evening in company with Colonel Wilson, Grant's inspector general.

The next morning I went to see General Thomas; it was not an official visit, but a friendly one, such a visit as I very often made on the generals. When we had shaken hands, he said:

"Mr. Dana, you have got me this time; but there is nothing for a man to do in such a case as this but to obey orders."

This was in allusion to his assignment to the command of the Army of the Cumberland. The change in command was received with satisfaction by all intelligent officers, so far as I could ascertain, though, of course, Rosecrans had many friends who were unable to conceive why he was relieved. They reported that he was to be put in command of the Army of the Potomac. The change at headquarters was already strikingly perceptible, order prevailing instead of universal chaos.

On the evening of the 23d Grant arrived, as I stated in my dispatch to Mr. Stanton, "wet, dirty, and well." The next morning he was out with Thomas and Smith to reconnoiter a position which the latter general had discovered at the mouth of Lookout Valley, which he believed, if it could be taken possession of and at the same time if Raccoon Mountain could be occupied, would give us Lookout Valley, and so enable us again to bring supplies up the river. In preparation for this movement, Smith had been getting bridges ready to throw across the river at the mouth of the valley, and been fitting up a steamer to use for supplies when we should control the river.

The Confederates at that time were massed in Chattanooga Valley, south of Chattanooga. They held Missionary Ridge to the east, and Lookout Mountain to the west. They had troops in Lookout Valley also, and their pickets extended westward over Raccoon Mountain to the river. South of the river, at Brown's Ferry, were several low mamelons. Smith's idea was to surprise the Confederate pickets here at night and seize the position in time to unite with Hooker, who in the meantime should be ordered up from Bridgeport by way of Shellmound, Whiteside, and Wauhatchie. That night Grant gave orders for the movement; in fact, he began it by sending Palmer's division across Walden's Ridge to Rankin's Ferry, where he was to cross and occupy Shellmound, thus guarding Hooker's rear. Hooker he ordered to march from Bridgeport on the morning of the 26th.

I went to Bridgeport on the 25th to observe Hooker's movement, but found he was not there, and would not be ready to march the next morning as ordered. Hooker came up from Stevenson to Bridgeport on the evening of the 26th. He was in an unfortunate state of mind for one who had to co-operate—fault-finding and criticizing. No doubt it was true that the chaos of the Rosecrans administration was as bad as he described it to be, but he was quite as truculent toward the plan that he was now to execute as toward the impotence and confusion of the old regime. By the next morning he was ready to start, and the troops moved out for Shellmound about half past six. By half past four in the afternoon we arrived at Whiteside Valley; thence the march was directly to Wauhatchie. Here there was an insignificant skirmish, which did not stop us long. By the afternoon of the 28th we were at the mouth of the Lookout Valley, where we found that General Smith, by an operation whose brilliancy cannot be exaggerated, had taken the mamelons south of the river.

The only serious opposition to our occupancy of the position came that night, but the enemy was successfully repulsed.

Our forces now held Lookout Valley and controlled the river from Brown's Ferry to Bridgeport. The next day supplies were started up the river. At first they came no farther than Kelley's Ferry, which was about ten miles from Chattanooga. This was because the steamer at Bridgeport could not get through the Suck, an ugly pass in the mountains through which the river runs; but on the night of the 30th we succeeded in getting our steamer at Chattanooga past the pickets on Lookout Mountain and down to Brown's Ferry. She could pass the Suck, and after that supplies came by water to Brown's Ferry.

Within a week after Grant's arrival we were receiving supplies daily. There was no further danger of the Army of the Cumberland being starved out of Chattanooga. The Confederates themselves at once recognized this, for a copy of the Atlanta Appeal of November 3d which reached me said that if we were not dislodged from Lookout Valley our possession of Chattanooga was secure for the winter.

It was now certain that we could hold Chattanooga; but until Sherman reached us we could do nothing against the enemy and nothing to relieve Burnside, who had been ordered to unite with Rosecrans in August, but had never got beyond Knoxville. He was shut up there much in the same way as we were in Chattanooga, and it was certain that the Confederates were sending forces against him.

The day after Grant arrived we had good evidence that the Confederates were moving in large force to the northeastward of Chattanooga, for heavy railroad trains went out in that direction and light ones returned. Deserters to us on the morning of the 25th<reported that a large force was at Charleston, Tenn., and that fully five thousand mounted infantry had crossed the Tennessee River above Washington. That night it was noticed that the pickets on Lookout Mountain, and even down into the valley on the Chattanooga side, were much diminished. We judged from this that the enemy had withdrawn both from the top of the mountain and from the valley. There were other rumors of their movements toward Burnside during the next few days,

and on November 6th some definite information came through a deserter, a Northern man who had lived in Georgia before the war and had been forced into the service. He reported that two divisions had moved up the Tennessee some time ago, and confirmed our suspicion that the troops had been withdrawn from Lookout Mountain. He said it was well understood among the Confederates that these forces were going by way of Loudon to join those which had already gone up the river, to co-operate with a force of Lee's army in driving Burnside out of East Tennessee.

Grant's first move to meet this plan of the enemy was to direct Sherman, who had been trying to rebuild and hold the railroad from Memphis as he marched forward, to abandon this work and hasten up to Stevenson. Grant then considered what movement could be made which would compel the enemy to recall the troops sent against Burnside.

Grant was so anxious to know the real condition of Burnside that he asked me to go to Knoxville and find out. So on November 9th I started, accompanied by Colonel Wilson of Grant's staff. The way in which such a trip as this of Wilson and mine was managed in those days is told in this letter to a child, written just before we left Chattanooga for Knoxville:

> I expect to go all the way on horseback, and it will take about five days. About seventy horsemen will go along with their sabers and carbines to keep off the guerillas. Our baggage we shall have carried on pack mules. These are funny little rats of creatures, with the big panniers fastened to their sides to carry their burdens in. I shall put my bed in one pannier and my carpet bag and India-rubber things in the other. Colonel Wilson, who is to go with me, will have another mule for his traps, and a third will carry the bread and meat and coffee that we are to live on. At night we shall halt in some nice shady nook where there is a spring, build a big roaring fire, cook our supper, spread our blankets on the ground, and sleep with our feet toward the fire, while half a dozen of the soldiers, with their guns ready loaded, watch all about to keep the rebels at a safe distance. Then in the morning we shall first wake up, then wash our faces, get our breakfasts, and march on, like John Brown's soul, toward our

destination. How long I shall stay at Knoxville is uncertain, but I hope not very long—though it must be very charming in that country of mountains and rivers—and then I shall pray for orders that will take me home again.

We were not obliged to camp out every night on this trip. One evening, just about supper time, we reached a large stone house, the home of a farmer. The man, we found, was a strong Unionist, and he gave us a hearty invitation to occupy his premises. Our escort took possession of the barn for sleeping, and we cooked our supper in the yard, the family lending us a table and sending us out fresh bread. After supper Wilson and I were invited into the house, where the farmer listened eagerly to the news of the Union army. There were two or three young and very pretty girls in the farmer's family, and while we talked they dipped snuff, a peculiar custom that I had seen but once or twice before.

Wilson also notes this in his memoir, writing that even the family's small children dipped snuff.—Ed. 2018

We reached Knoxville on the 13th, and I at once went to headquarters to talk over the situation with Burnside. This was the first time I had met that general. He was rather a large man physically, about six feet tall, with a large face and a small head, and heavy side whiskers. He was an energetic, decided man, frank, manly, and well educated. He was a very showy officer—not that he made any show; he was naturally that. When he first talked with you, you would think he had a great deal more intelligence than he really possessed. You had to know him some time before you really took his measure.

I found that Burnside's forces, something like thirty-three thousand men of all arms, were scattered all the way from Kentucky, by Cumberland Gap, down to Knoxville. In and about Knoxville he had not concentrated more than twelve thousand to fourteen thousand men. The town was fortified, though unable to resist an attack by a large force. Up to this time Burnside and his army had really been very well off, for he had commanded a rich region behind Knoxville, and thence had drawn food and forage. He even had about one hundred miles of railroad in active operation for foraging, and he had plenty of mills and workshops in the town which he could use.

After a detailed conversation with Burnside, I concluded that there was no reason to believe that any force had been sent from Lee's army to attack him on the northeast, as we had heard in Chattanooga, but that it was certain that Longstreet was approaching from Chattanooga with thirty thousand troops. Burnside said that he would be unable long to resist such an attack, and that if Grant did not succeed in making a demonstration which would compel Longstreet to return he must retreat.

If compelled to retreat, he proposed, he said, to follow the line of Cumberland Gap, and to hold Morristown and Bean's Station. At these points he would be secure against any force the enemy could bring against him; he would still be able to forage over a large extent of country on the south and east, he could prevent the repair of the railroads by the rebels, and he would still have an effective hold on East Tennessee.

A few hours after this talk with Burnside, about one o'clock in the morning of the 14th, a report reached Knoxville that completely upset his plan for retreating by Cumberland Gap. This was the news that the enemy had commenced building bridges across the Tennessee near Loudon, only about twenty-five miles south of Knoxville. Burnside immediately decided that he must retreat; and he actually dictated orders for drawing his whole army south of the Holston into Blount County, where all his communications would have been cut off, and where on his own estimate he could not have subsisted more than three weeks. General Parke argued against this in vain, but finally Colonel Wilson overcame it by representing that Grant did not wish Burnside to include the capture of his entire army among the plans of his operations. He then determined to retreat toward the gaps, after destroying the workshops and mills in Knoxville and on the line of his march.

Before we left, however, which was about six o'clock in the morning of the 14th, General Burnside had begun to feel that perhaps he might not be obliged to pass the mountains and abandon East Tennessee entirely. He had even decided to send out a force to attack the enemy's advance. When Wilson and I reached Lenoir's Station that morning on our way to Chattanooga, we discovered that the enemy's attack was not as imminent as Burnside feared. Their bridges were not complete, and no artillery or cavalry had crossed. From everything I could learn of their strength, in fact, it seemed to me that there was a reasonable probability that Burnside would be able to hold Knoxville until relieved by operations at Chattanooga.

We found that our departure from Knoxville had been none too soon. So completely were the Confederates taking possession of the country between Knoxville and Chattanooga that had we delayed a single day we could have got out only through Cumberland Gap or that of Big Creek. We were four days in returning, and Mr. Stanton became very uneasy, as I learned from this dispatch received soon after my return:

War Department,

Washington, D. C., November 19, 1863.

Hon. C. A. Dana, Chattanooga.

Your dispatches of yesterday are received. I am rejoiced that you have got safely back. My anxiety about you for several days had been very great. Make your arrangements to remain in the field during the winter. Continue your reports as frequently as possible, always noting the hour.

Edwin M. Stanton.

Colonel Wilson and I reached Chattanooga on November 17th. As soon as I arrived I went to Grant's and Thomas's headquarters to find out the news. There was the greatest hopefulness everywhere. Sherman, they told me, had reached Bridgeport, and a plan for attacking Bragg's position was complete and its execution begun by moving a division of Sherman's army from Bridgeport to Trenton, where it ought to arrive that day, threatening the enemy by Stevens's Gap. The remainder of that army was to move into Lookout Valley by way of Whiteside, extending its lines up the valley toward Trenton, as if to repeat the flanking movement of Rosecrans when he followed Bragg across the Tennessee. Having drawn the enemy's attention to that quarter, Sherman was to disappear on the night of the 18th and encamp his forces behind the ridge of hills north of the Tennessee, opposite to Chattanooga, and keep them there out of sight of the enemy during the 19th. That same night a bridge was to be thrown across the river just below the mouth of Chickamauga Creek, so that on Saturday morning, November 20th, Sherman's command would be across before daylight, if possible. As soon as over he was to push for the head of Missionary Ridge, and there engage the enemy.

At the same time that Sherman's wing advanced, Granger, with about eighteen thousand men, was to move up on the left of the Chattanooga lines and engage the Confederate right with all possible vigor. Hooker, who had been in the Lookout Valley ever since he joined the army in November, was to attack the head of Lookout Mountain simultaneously with Sherman's attack at the head of Missionary Ridge, and, if practicable, to carry the mountain.

It is almost never possible to execute a campaign as laid out, especially when it requires so many concerted movements as this one. Thus, instead of all of Sherman's army crossing the Tennessee on the night of the 18th, and getting out of sight as expected behind the hills that night, a whole corps was left behind at daylight, and one division had to march down the valley on the morning of the 20th in full view of the enemy, who now understood, of course, that he was to be attacked. Bragg evidently did not care to risk a battle, for he tried to alarm Grant that afternoon by sending a flag over, and with it a letter, saying, "As there may still be some non-combatants in Chattanooga, I deem it proper to notify you that prudence would dictate their early withdrawal." Of course, we all knew this was a bluff.

On the morning of the 20th a heavy rain began, which lasted two days and made the roads so bad that Sherman's advance was almost stopped. His march was still further retarded by a singular blunder which had been committed in moving his forces from Bridgeport. Instead of moving all the troops and artillery first, the numerous trains which had been brought from West Tennessee were sent in front rather than in rear of each division. Grant said the blunder was his; that he should have given Sherman explicit orders to leave his wagons behind; but no one was so much astonished as Grant on learning that they had not been left, even without such orders.

Owing to these unforeseen circumstances, Sherman's rear was so far behind on the morning of the 23d, three days after Grant had planned for the attack, that it was doubtful whether he could be ready to join the movement the next day, November 24th. It was also feared that the enemy, who had seen the troops march through Lookout Valley and then disappear, might have discovered where they were concealed, and thus surmise our movements.

On account of these hitches in carrying out the operations as speedily as Grant had hoped, it was not until November 23d that the first encounter in the battle of Chattanooga occurred. It was the beginning of the most spectacular military operations I ever saw—operations extending over three days and full of the most exciting incidents.

Our army lay to the south and east of the town of Chattanooga, the river being at our back. Facing us, in a great half circle, and high above us on Lookout Mountain and Missionary Ridge, were the Confederates. Our problem was to drive them from these heights. We had got our men well together, all the re-enforcements were up, and now we were to strike.

The first thing Grant tried to do was to clear out the Confederate lines which were nearest to ours on the plain south of Chattanooga, and to get hold of two bald knobs, or low hills, where Bragg's forces had their advance guard. As the entire field where this attack was to be made was distinctly visible from one of our forts, I went there on the 23d with the generals to watch the operations. The troops employed for the attack were under the immediate orders of Gordon Granger. There were some capital officers under Granger, among them Sheridan, Hazen, and T. J. Wood. Just before one o'clock the men moved out of their entrenchments, and remained in line for three quarters of an hour in full view of the enemy. The spectacle was one of singular magnificence.

Our point of view was Fort Wood. Usually in a battle one sees only a little corner of what is going on, the movements near where you happen to be; but in the battle of Chattanooga we had the whole scene before us. At last, everything being ready, Granger gave the order to advance, and three brigades of men pushed out simultaneously. The troops advanced rapidly, with all the precision of a review, the flags flying and the bands playing. The first sign of a battle one noticed was the fire spitting out of the rifles of the skirmishers. The lines moved steadily along, not halting at all, the skirmishers all the time advancing in front, firing and receiving fire.

The first shot was fired at two o'clock, and in five minutes Hazen's skirmishers were briskly engaged, while the artillery of Forts Wood and Thomas was opening upon the rebel rifle-pits and camps behind the line of fighting. The practice of our gunners was splendid, but it elicited no reply from the camps and batteries of the enemy, about a mile and three quarters distant; and it was soon evident that the Confederates had no heavy artillery, in that part of their lines at least. Our troops, rapidly advancing toward the knobs upon which they were directed, occupied them at twenty minutes past two. Ten minutes later Samuel Beatty, who commanded a brigade, driving forward across an open field, carried the rifle-pits in his front, the occupants fleeing as they fired their last volley; and Sheridan, moving through the forest which stretched before him, drove in the enemy's pickets. Sheridan halted his advance, in obedience to orders, on reaching the rifle-pits, where the rebel force was waiting for his attack. No such attack was made, however, the design being to secure only the height. The entire movement was carried out in such an incredibly short time that at half past three

I was able to send a telegram to Mr. Stanton describing the victory.

We took about two hundred prisoners, mostly Alabama troops, and had gained a position which would be of great importance should the enemy still attempt to hold the Chattanooga Valley. With these heights in our possession, a column marching to turn Missionary Ridge was secure from flank attack. The Confederates fired three small guns only during the affair, and that tended to confirm the impression that they had withdrawn their main force. About four o'clock in the afternoon the enemy opened fire from the top of Missionary Ridge, the total number of cannon they displayed being about twelve, but nothing was developed to show decisively whether they would fight or flee. Grant thought the latter; other judicious officers the former.

That evening I left Chattanooga to join General Sherman, who had his troops north of the river concealed behind the hills, and ready to attempt to cross the Tennessee that very night, so as to be able to attack the east head of Missionary Ridge on the night of the 24th or the morning of the 25th.

Sherman had some twenty-five thousand men, and crossing them over a river as wide and rapid as the Tennessee was above Chattanooga seemed to me a serious task, and I watched the operations of the night with great curiosity. The first point was to get a sufficient body of troops on the south bank to hold a position against the enemy (the Confederates had pickets for a long distance up and down the Tennessee, above Chattanooga), and then from there commence building the pontoon bridge by which the bulk of the men were to be got over.

About one o'clock in the morning the pontoon boats, which had been sent up the river some distance, were filled with men and allowed to drop down to the point General Sherman had chosen for the south end of his bridge. They landed about 2.30 in the morning, seized the pickets, and immediately began to fortify their position. The boats in the meantime were sent across the river to bring over fresh loads of men. They kept this up until morning. Then a small steamer which Sherman had got hold of came up and began to bring over troops. At daybreak some of the boats were taken from the ferrying and a bridge was begun. It was marvelous with what vigor the work went on. Sherman told me he had never seen anything done so quietly and so well, and he declared later in his report that he did not believe the history of war could show a bridge of that length—about thirteen hundred and fifty feet—laid down so noiselessly and in so short a time. By one o'clock in the afternoon (November 24th) the bridge was done, and the balance of his forces were soon marching briskly across. As soon as Sherman saw that the crossing was insured, he set the foremost of his column in motion for the head of Missionary Ridge. By four o'clock he had gained the crest of the ridge and was preparing for the next day's battle.

As soon as I saw Sherman in position, I hurried back to Chattanooga. I reached there just in time to see the famous moonlight battle on Lookout Mountain. The way this night battle happened to be fought was that Hooker, who had been holding Lookout Valley, had been ordered to gain a foothold on Lookout Mountain if possible, and that day, while I was with Sherman, had really succeeded in scaling the side of the mountain. But his possession of the point he had reached had been so hotly disputed that a brigade had been sent from Chattanooga to aid him. These troops attacked the Confederate lines on the eastern slope of the mountain about eight o'clock that evening. A full moon made the battlefield as plain to us in the valley as if it were day, the blaze of their camp fires and the flashes of their guns displaying brilliantly their position and the progress of their advance. No report of the result was received that night, but the next morning we knew that Bragg had evacuated Lookout Mountain the night before, and that our troops occupied it.

After the successes of the two days a decisive battle seemed inevitable, and orders were given that night for a vigorous attack the next morning. I was up early, sending my first dispatch to Mr. Stanton at half past seven o'clock. As the result of the operations of the day before, Grant held the point of Lookout Mountain on the southwest and the crest of the east end of Missionary Ridge, and his line was continuous between these points. As the result of the movement on November 23d, our lines in front had been advanced to Orchard Knob. The bulk of the Confederate force was entrenched along Missionary Ridge, five to six hundred feet above us, and facing our center and left. From Chattanooga we could see the full length of our own and the enemy's lines spread out like a scene in a theater.

About nine o'clock the battle was commenced on Sherman's line on our left, and it raged furiously all that forenoon both east of Missionary Ridge and along its crest, the enemy making vigorous efforts to crush Sherman and dislodge him from his position on the ridge. All day, while this battle was going on, I was at Orchard Knob, where Grant, Thomas, Granger, and several other officers were observing the operations. The enemy kept firing shells at us, I remember, from the ridge opposite. They had got the range so well that the shells burst pretty near the top of the elevation where we were, and when we saw them coming we would duck—that is, everybody did except Generals Grant and Thomas and Gordon Granger. It was not according to their dignity to go down on their marrow bones. While we were there Granger got a cannon—how he got it I do not know—and he would load it with the help of one soldier and fire it himself over at the ridge. I recollect that Rawlins was very much disgusted at the guerilla operations of Granger, and induced Grant to order him to join his troops elsewhere.

As we thought we perceived, soon after noon, that the enemy had sent a great mass of their troops to crush Sherman, Grant gave orders at two o'clock for an assault upon the left of their lines; but owing to the fault of Granger, who was boyishly intent upon firing his gun instead of commanding his corps, Grant's order was not transmitted to the division commanders until he repeated it an hour later.

It was fully four o'clock before the line moved out to the attack. It was a bright, sunny afternoon, and, as the forces marched across the valley in front of us as regularly as if on parade, it was a great spectacle. They took with ease the first rifle-pits at the foot of the ridge as they had been ordered, and then, to the amazement of all of us who watched on Orchard Knob, they moved out and up the steep ahead of them, and before we realized it they were at the top of Missionary Ridge. It was just half past four when I wired to Mr. Stanton:

> Glory to God! the day is decisively ours. Missionary Ridge has just been carried by the magnificent charge of Thomas's troops, and the rebels routed.

As soon as Grant saw the ridge was ours, he started for the front. As he rode the length of the lines, the men, who were frantic with joy and enthusiasm over the victory, received him with tumultuous shouts. The storming of the ridge by our troops was one of the greatest miracles in military history. No man who climbs the ascent by any of the roads that wind along its front can believe that eighteen thousand men were moved in tolerably good order up its broken and crumbling face unless it was his fortune to witness the deed. It seemed as awful as a visible interposition of God. Neither Grant nor Thomas intended it. Their orders were to carry the rifle-pits along the base of the ridge and capture their occupants; but when this was accomplished, the unaccountable spirit of the troops bore them bodily up those impracticable steeps, in spite of the bristling rifle-pits on the crest, and the thirty cannons enfilading every gully. The order to storm appears to have been given simultaneously by Generals Sheridan and Wood because the men were not to be held back, dangerous as the attempt appeared to military prudence. Besides, the generals had caught the inspiration of the men, and were ready themselves to undertake impossibilities.

The first time I saw Sheridan after the battle I said to him, "Why did you go up there?"

"When I saw the men were going up" he replied, "I had no idea of stopping them; the rebel pits had been taken and nobody had been hurt, and after they had started I commanded them to go right on. I looked up at the head of the ridge as I was going up, and there I saw a Confederate general on horseback. I had a silver whisky flask in my pocket, and when I saw this man on the top of the hill I took out my flask and waved my hand toward him, holding up the shining, glittering flask, and then I took a drink. He waved back to me, and then the whole corps went up."

All the evening of the 25th the excitement of the battle continued. Bragg had retreated down the Chickamauga Valley and was burning what he could not carry away, so that the east was lit by his fires, while Sheridan continued his fight along the east slope of Missionary Ridge until nine o'clock in the evening. It was a bright moonlight night, and we could see most of the operations as plainly as by day. The next morning1 Bragg was in full retreat. I went to Missionary Ridge in the morning, and from there I could see along ten miles of Chickamauga Valley the fires of the depots and bridges he was burning as he fled.

At intervals throughout the day I sent dispatches to Washington, where they were eagerly read, as the following telegram sent me on the 27th shows:

War Department,

Washington City, November 27, 1863.

Hon. C. A. Dana, Chattanooga, Tenn.:

The Secretary of War is absent and the President is sick, but both receive your dispatches regularly and esteem them highly, not merely because they are reliable, but for their clearness of narrative and their graphic pictures of the stirring events they describe.

The patient endurance and spirited valor exhibited by commanders and men in the last great feat of arms, which has crowned our cause with such a glorious success, is making all of us hero worshipers.

P. H. Watson,

Acting Secretary of War.

Lincoln had recently returned from giving his famous address at Gettysburg on the 19th and was suffering from what was then termed "varaloid," a mild form of smallpox.—Ed. 2018

The enemy was now divided. Bragg was flying toward Rome and Atlanta, and Longstreet was in East Tennessee besieging

Burnside. Our victorious army was between them. The first thought was, of course, to relieve Burnside, and Grant ordered Granger with the Fourth Corps instantly forward to his aid, taking pains to write Granger a personal letter, explaining the exigencies of the case and the imperative need of energy. It had no effect, however, in hastening the movement, and a day or two later Grant ordered Sherman to assume command of all the forces operating from the south to save Knoxville. Grant became imbued with a strong prejudice against Granger from this circumstance.

As any movement against Bragg was impracticable at that season, the only operations possible to Grant, beyond the relief of Burnside, were to hold Chattanooga and the line of the Hiwassee, to complete and protect the railroads and the steamboats upon the Tennessee, and to amass food, forage, and ordnance stores for the future. But all this would require only a portion of the forces under his command; and, instead of holding the remainder in winter quarters, he evolved a plan to employ them in an offensive winter campaign against Mobile and the interior of Alabama. He asked me to lay his plan before Mr. Stanton, and urge its approval by the Government, which, of course, I did at once by telegraph.

I did not wait at Chattanooga to learn the decision of the Government on Grant's plan, but left on November 29th, again with Colonel Wilson, to join Sherman, now well on his way to Knoxville, and to observe his campaign.

I fell in with Sherman on November 30th at Charleston, on the Hiwassee. The Confederate guard there fled at his approach, after half destroying the bridges, and we had to stay there until one was repaired. When we reached Loudon, on December 3d, the bridge over the Tennessee was gone, so that the main body of the army marched to a point where it was believed a practicable ford might be found. The ford, however, proved too deep for the men, the river being two hundred yards wide, and the water almost at freezing point. We had a great deal of fun getting across. I remember my horse went through—swam through, where his feet could not strike the ground—and I got across without any difficulty. I think Wilson got across, too; but when the lieutenant of our squad of cavalrymen got in the middle of the river, where it was so deep that as he sat in the saddle the water came up to his knees almost, and a little above the breast of the mule he rode, the animal turned his head upward toward the current, at that place very strong, and would not stir. This poor fellow sat there in the middle of the stream, and, do his best, he could not move his beast. Finally, they drove in a big wagon, or truck, with two horses, and tied that to the bits of the mule, and dragged him out.

Colonel Wilson at once set about the construction of a trestle bridge, and by working all night had it so advanced that the troops could begin to cross by daylight the next morning.

While the crossing was going on, we captured a Confederate mail, and first learned something authentic about Burnside. He had been assailed by Longstreet on the 29th of November, but had repulsed him. He was still besieged, and all the letter writers spoke of the condition in the town with great despondency, evidently regarding their chance of extrication as very poor. Longstreet, we gathered from the mail, thought that Sherman was bringing up only a small force.

By noon of December 5th we had our army over, and, as we were now only thirty-five miles from Knoxville, we pushed ahead rapidly, the enemy making but little resistance. When Longstreet discovered the strength of our force he retreated, and we entered Knoxville at noon on the 6th. We found to our surprise that General Burnside had fully twenty days' provisions—much more, in fact, than at the beginning of the siege. These supplies had been drawn from the French Broad by boats, and by the Sevierville road. The loyal people of East Tennessee had done their utmost through the whole time to send in provisions and forage, and Longstreet left open the very avenues which Burnside most desired. We found ammunition very short, and projectiles for our rifle guns had been made in the town. The utmost constancy and unanimity had prevailed during the whole siege, from Burnside down to the last private; no man thought of retreat or surrender.

The next morning after our arrival, December 7th, Sherman started back to Chattanooga with all his force not needed there. Colonel Wilson and I returned with him, reaching Chattanooga on December 10th.

Everything in the army was now so safe, quiet, and regular that I felt I could be more useful anywhere else, so the day I got back I asked leave of Mr. Stanton to go North. I did not wait for his reply, however. The morning of the 12th Grant sent for me to come to his headquarters, and asked me to go to Washington to represent more fully to Stanton and Halleck his wishes with regard to the winter campaign. As the matter was important, I started at once, telegraphing Mr. Stanton that, if he thought it unnecessary for me to go, orders would reach me at any point on the railroad.

THE WAR DEPARTMENT IN WAR TIMES

I reached Washington about the middle of December, and immediately gave to Mr. Stanton an outline of Grant's plan and reasons for a winter campaign. The President, Mr. Stanton, and General Halleck all agreed that the proposed operations were the most promising in sight; indeed, Mr. Stanton was enthusiastic in favor of the scheme as I presented it to him. He said that the success of Grant's campaign would end the war in the Mississippi Valley, and practically make prisoners of all the rebel forces in the interior of Mississippi and Alabama, without our being at the direct necessity of guarding and feeding them. But Halleck, as a sine qua non, insisted that East Tennessee should first be cleared out and Longstreet driven off permanently and things up to date secured, before new campaigns were entered upon.

The result was that no winter campaign was made in 1863-64 toward the Alabama River towns and Mobile. Its success, in my opinion, was certain, and I so represented to Mr. Stanton. Without jeoparding our interests in any other quarter, Grant would have opened the Alabama River and captured Mobile a full year before it finally fell. Its success meant permanent security for everything we had already laid hold of, at once freeing many thousands of garrison troops for service elsewhere. As long as the rebels held Alabama, they had a base from which to strike Tennessee. I had unbounded confidence in Grant's skill and energy to conduct such a campaign into the interior, cutting loose entirely from his base and subsisting off the enemy's country. At the time he had the troops, and could have finished the job in three months.

After I had explained fully my mission from Grant, I asked the Secretary what he wanted me to do. Mr. Stanton told me he would like to have me remain in the department until I was needed again at the front. Accordingly, an office in the War Department was provided for me, and I began to do the regular work of an assistant to the Secretary of War. This was the first time since my relations with the War Department began that I had been thrown much with the Secretary, and I was very glad to have an opportunity to observe him.

Mr. Stanton was a short, thick, dark man, with a very large head and a mass of black hair. His nature was intense, and he was one of the most eloquent men that I ever met. Stanton was entirely absorbed in his duties, and his energy in prosecuting them was some- thing almost superhuman. When he took hold of the War Department the armies seemed to grow, and they certainly gained in force and vim and thoroughness.

One of the first things which struck me in Mr. Stanton was his deep religious feeling and his familiarity with the Bible. He must have studied the Bible a great deal when he was a boy. He had the firmest conviction that the Lord directed our armies. Over and over again have I heard him express the same opinion which he wrote to the *Tribune* after Donelson: "Much has recently been said of military combinations and organizing victory. I hear such phrases with apprehension. They commenced in infidel France with the Italian campaign, and resulted in Waterloo. Who can organize victory? Who can combine the elements of success on the battlefield? We owe our recent victories to the Spirit of the Lord, that moved our soldiers to rush into battle, and filled the hearts of our enemies with dismay. The inspiration that conquered in battle was in the hearts of the soldiers and from on high; and wherever there is the same inspiration there will be the same results." There was never any cant in Stanton's religious feeling. It was the straightforward expression of what he believed and lived, and was as simple and genuine and real to him as the principles of his business.

Stanton was a serious student of history. He had read many books on the subject—more than on any other, I should say—and he was fond of discussing historical characters with his associates; not that he made a show of his learning. He was fond, too, of discussing legal questions, and would listen with eagerness to the statement of cases in which friends had been interested. He was a man who was devoted to his friends, and he had a good many with whom he liked to sit down and talk. In conversation he was witty and satirical; he told a story well, and was very companionable.

There is a popular impression that Mr. Stanton took a malevolent delight in browbeating his subordinates, and even now and then making a spectacle of some poor officer or soldier, who unfortunately fell into his clutches in the Secretary's reception room, for the edification of bystanders. This idea, like many other false notions concerning great men, is largely a mistaken one. The stories which are told of Mr. Stanton's impatience and violence are exaggerated. He could speak in a very peremptory tone, but I never heard him say anything that could be called vituperative.

There were certain men in whom he had little faith, and I have heard him speak to some of these in a tone of severity. He was a man of the quickest intelligence, and understood a thing before half of it was told him. His judgment was just as swift, and when he got hold of a man who did not understand, who did not state his case clearly, he was very impatient.

If Stanton liked a man, he was always pleasant. I was with him for several years in the most confidential relations, and I can now recall only one instance of his speaking to me in a harsh tone. It was a curious case. Among the members of Congress at that period was a Jew named Strouse. One of Strouse's race, who lived in Virginia, had gone down to the mouth of the James River when General Butler was at Fortress Monroe, and had announced his wish to leave the Confederacy. Now, the orders were that when a man came to a commanding officer with a request to go through the lines, he was to be examined and all the money he had was to be taken from him. General Butler had taken from this Virginian friend of Strouse between fifty thousand and seventy-five thousand dollars. When a general took money in this way he had to deposit it at once in the Treasury; there a strict account was kept of the amount, whom it was taken by, and whom it was taken from. Butler gave a receipt to this man, and he afterward came to Washington to get his money. He and Strouse came to the War

Department, where they bothered Mr. Stanton a good deal. Finally, Mr. Stanton sent for me.

"Strouse is after me," he said ; "he wants that money, and I want you to settle the matter."

"What shall I do?" I asked ; "what are the orders?" He took the papers in the case and wrote on the back of them:

> Referred to Mr. Dana, Assistant Secretary of War, to be settled as in his judgment shall be best.
>
> E. M. Stanton.

The man then turned his attention from the Secretary to me. I looked into the matter, and gave him back the money. The next day Mr. Stanton sent for me. I saw he was angry.

"Did you give that Jew back his money?" he asked in a harsh tone.

"Yes, sir."

"Well," he said, "I should like to know by what authority you did it."

"If you will excuse me while I go to my room, I will show my authority to you," I replied.

So I went up and brought down the paper he had indorsed, and read to him:

"Referred to Mr. Dana, Assistant Secretary of War, to be settled as in his judgment shall be best." Then I handed it over to him. He looked at it, and then he laughed.

"You are right," he said; "you have got me this time." That was the only time he spoke to me in a really harsh tone.

At the time that I entered the War Department for regular duty, it was a very busy place. Mr. Stanton frequently worked late at night, keeping his carriage waiting for him. I never worked at night, as my eyes would not allow it. I got to my office about nine o'clock in the morning, and I stayed there nearly the whole day, for I made it a rule never to go away until my desk was cleared.

When I arrived I usually found on my table a big pile of papers which were to be acted on, papers of every sort that had come to me from the different departments of the office.

The business of the War Department during the first winter that I spent in Washington was something enormous. Nearly $285,000,000 [about $4,400,000,000 in 2015] was paid out that year (from June, 1863, to June, 1864) by the quartermaster's office, and $221,000,000 stood in accounts at the end of the year awaiting examination before payment was made. We had to buy every conceivable 13   161 thing that an army of men could need. We bought fuel, forage, furniture, coffins, medicine, horses, mules, telegraph wire, sugar, coffee, flour, cloth, caps, guns, powder, and thousands of other things. Sometimes our supplies came by contract; again by direct purchase; again by manufacture. Of course, by the fall of 1863 the army was pretty well supplied; still, that year we bought over 3,000,000 pairs of trousers, nearly 5,000,000 flannel shirts and drawers, some 7,000,000 pairs of stockings, 325,000 mess pans, 207,000 camp kettles, over 13,000 drums, and 14,830 fifes. It was my duty to make contracts for many of these supplies.

In making contracts for supplies of all kinds, we were obliged to take careful precautions against frauds.

I had a colleague in the department, the Hon. Peter H. Watson, the distinguished patent lawyer, who had a great knack at detecting army frauds. One which Watson had spent much time in trying to ferret out came to light soon after I went into office. This was an extensive fraud in forage furnished to the Army of the Potomac. The trick of the fraud consisted in a dishonest mixture of oats and Indian corn for the horses and mules of the army. By changing the proportions of the two sorts of grain, the contractors were able to make a considerable difference in the cost of the bushel, on account of the difference in the weight and price of the grain, and it was difficult to detect the cheat. However, Watson found it out, and at once arrested the men who were most directly involved.

Soon after the arrest Watson went to New York. While he was gone, certain parties from Philadelphia interested in the swindle came to me at the War Department. Among them was the president of the Corn Exchange. They paid me thirty-three thousand dollars to cover the sum which one of the men confessed he had appropriated; thirty-two thousand dollars was the amount restored by another individual. The morning after this transaction the Philadelphians returned to me, demanding both that the villains should be released, and that the papers and funds belonging to them, taken at the time of their arrest, should be restored. It was my judgment that, instead of being released, they should be remanded to solitary confinement until they could clear up all the forage frauds and make complete justice possible. Then I should have released them, but not before. So I telegraphed to Watson what had happened, and asked him to return to prevent any false step.

Now, it happened that the men arrested were of some political importance in Pennsylvania, and eminent politicians took a hand in getting them out of the scrape. Among others, the Hon. David Wilmot, then Senator of the United States and author of the famous Wilmot proviso, was very active. He went to Mr. Lincoln and made such representations and appeals that finally the President consented to go with him over to the War Department and see Watson in his office. Wilmot remained outside, and Mr. Lincoln went in to labor with the Assistant Secretary. Watson eloquently described the nature of the fraud, and the extent to which it had already been developed by his partial investigation. The President, in reply, dwelt upon the fact that a large amount of money had been refunded by the guilty men, and urged the greater question of the safety of the cause and the necessity of preserving united the powerful support which Pennsylvania was giving to the administration in suppressing the rebellion. Watson answered:

"Very well, Mr. President, if you wish to have these men released, all that is necessary is to give the order; but I shall ask to have it in writing. In such a case as this it would not be safe for me to obey a verbal order; and let me add that if you do release them the fact and the reason will necessarily become known to the people."

Finally Mr. Lincoln took up his hat and went out. Wilmot was waiting in the corridor, and came to meet him.

"Wilmot," he said, "I can't do anything with Watson; he won't release them."

The reply which the Senator made to this remark cannot be printed here, but it did not affect the judgment or the action of the President.

The men were retained for a long time afterward. The fraud was fully investigated, and future swindles of the kind were rendered impossible. If Watson could have had his way, the guilty parties—and there were some whose names never got to the public—would have been tried by military commission and sternly dealt with. But my own reflections upon the subject led me to the conclusion that the moderation of the President was wiser than the unrelenting justice of the Assistant Secretary would have been.

Not a little of my time at the department was taken up with people who had missions of some kind within the lines of the army. I remember one of these particularly, because it brought me a characteristic letter from General Sherman. There was much suffering among the loyal citizens and the Quakers of East Tennessee in the winter of 1863-64, and many relief committees came to us seeking transportation and safe conduct for themselves and their supplies into that country. Some of these were granted, to the annoyance of General Sherman, then in command of the Military Division of the Mississippi. The reasons for his objections he gave in this letter to me:

Headquarters Military Division of the Mississippi,

Nashville, Tenn., April 21, 1864.

C. A. Dana, Esq., Ass't Sec. of War, Washington.

My dear Friend: It may be parliamentary, but is not military, for me to write you; but I feel assured anything I may write will only have the force of a casual conversation, such as we have indulged in by the camp fire or as we jogged along by the road. The text of my letter is one you gave a Philadelphia gentleman who is going up to East Tennessee to hunt up his brother Quakers and administer the bounties of his own and his fellow-citizens' charity. Now who would stand in the way of one so kindly and charitably disposed? Surely not I. But other questions present themselves. We have been working hard with tens of thousands of men, and at a cost of millions of dollars, to make railroads to carry to the line of the Tennessee enough provisions and material of war to enable us to push in our physical force to the next stop in the war. I have found on personal inspection that hitherto the railroads have barely been able to feed our men, that mules have died by the thousand, that arms and ammunition had [have] laid in the depot for two weeks for want of cars, that no accumulation at all of clothing and stores had been or could be moved at Chattanooga, and that it took four sets of cars and locomotives to accommodate the passes given by military commanders; that gradually the wants of citizens and charities were actually consuming the real resources of a road designed exclusively for army purposes. You have been on the spot and can understand my argument. At least one hundred citizens daily presented good claims to go forward—women to attend sick children, parents in search of the bodies of some slain in battle, sanitary committees sent by States and corporations to look after the personal wants of their constituents, ministers and friends to minister to the Christian wants of their flocks; men who had fled, anxious to go back to look after lost families, etc.; and, more still, the tons of goods which they all bore on their merciful errands. None but such as you, who have been present and seen the tens, hundreds, and thousands of such cases, can measure them in the aggregate and segregate the exceptions.

I had no time to hesitate, for but a short month was left me to prepare, and I must be ready to put in motion near one hundred thousand men to move when naught remains to save life. I figured up the mathematics, and saw that I must have daily one hundred and forty-five car loads of essentials for thirty days to enable me to fill the requirement. Only seventy-five daily was all the roads were doing. Now I have got it up to one hundred and thirty-five. Troops march, cattle go by the road, sanitary and sutler's stores limited, and all is done that human energy can accomplish. Yet come these pressing claims of charity, by men and women who cannot grasp the great problem. My usual answer is, "Show me that your presence at the front is more valuable than two hundred pounds of powder, bread, or oats"; and it is generally conclusive. I have given Mr. Savery a pass on your letter, and it takes two hundred pounds of bread from our soldiers, or the same of oats from our patient mules; but I could not promise to feed the suffering Quakers at the expense of our army. I have ordered all who cannot provide food at the front to be allowed transportation back in our empty cars; but I can not undertake to transport the food needed by the worthy East Tennesseans or any of them. In peace there is a beautiful harmony in all the departments of life—they all fit together like the Chinese puzzle; but in war all is ajar. Nothing fits, and it is the struggle between the stronger and weaker; and the latter, however it may appeal to the better feelings of our nature, must kick the beam. To make war we must and will harden our hearts.

Therefore, when preachers clamor and the sanitaries wail, don't join in, but know that war, like the thunderbolt, follows its laws, and turns not aside even if the beautiful, the virtuous, and charitable stand in its path.

When the day and the hour comes, I'll strike Joe Johnston, be the result what it may; but in the time allotted to me for preparation I must and will be selfish in making those preparations which I know to be necessary.

Your friend,

W. T. Sherman, Major General.

ABRAHAM LINCOLN AND HIS CABINET

During the first winter I spent in Washington in the War Department I had constant opportunities of seeing Mr. Lincoln, and of conversing with him in the cordial and unofficial manner which he always preferred. Not that there was ever any lack of dignity in the man. Even in his freest moments one always felt the presence of a will and of an intellectual power which maintained the ascendancy of his position. He never posed, or put on airs, or attempted to make any particular impression; but he was always conscious of his own ideas and purposes, even in his most unreserved moments.

I knew, too, and saw frequently, all the members of his Cabinet. When Mr. Lincoln was inaugurated as President, his first act was to name his Cabinet; and it was a common remark at the time that he had put into it every man who had competed with him for the nomination. The first in importance was William H. Seward, of New York, Mr. Lincoln's most prominent competitor. Mr. Seward was made Secretary of State. He was an interesting man, of an optimistic temperament, and he probably had the most cultivated and comprehensive intellect in the administration. He was a man who was all his life in controversies, yet he was singular in this, that, though forever in fights, he had almost no personal enemies. Seward had great ability as a writer, and he had what is very rare in a lawyer, a politician, or a statesman—imagination. A fine illustration of his genius was the acquisition of Alaska. That was one of the last things that he did before he went out of office, and it demonstrated more than anything else his fixed and never-changing idea that all North America should be united under one government.

Mr. Seward was an admirable writer and an impressive though entirely unpretentious speaker. He stood up and talked as though he were engaged in conversation, and the effect was always great. It gave the impression of a man deliberating "out loud" with himself.

The second man in importance and ability to be put into the Cabinet was Mr. Chase, of Ohio. He was an able, noble, spotless statesman, a man who would have been worthy of the best days of the old Roman republic. He had been a candidate for the presidency, though a less conspicuous one than Seward. Mr. Chase was a portly man; tall, and of an impressive appearance, with a very handsome, large head. He was genial, though very decided, and occasionally he would criticize the President, a thing I never heard Mr. Seward do. Chase had been successful in Ohio politics, and in the Treasury Department his administration was satisfactory to the public. He was the author of the national banking law. I remember going to dine with him one day—I did that pretty often, as I had known him well when I was on the *Tribune*—and he said to me: "I have completed today a very great thing. I have finished the National Bank Act. It will be a blessing to the country long after I am dead."

Chase famously had what Lincoln termed "White House fever" and considered running against his chief in 1864. Lincoln nominated him to the Supreme Court and he was confirmed. His daughter, Kate Chase Sprague, was one of the great belles of Civil War Washington.—Ed. 2018

The Secretary of the Navy throughout the war was Gideon Welles, of Connecticut. Welles was a curious-looking man: he wore a wig which was parted in the middle, the hair falling down on each side; and it was from his peculiar appearance, I have always thought, that the idea that he was an old fogy originated. I remember Governor Andrew, of Massachusetts, coming into my office at the War Department one day and asking where he could find "that old Mormon deacon, the Secretary of the Navy." In spite of his peculiarities, I think Mr. Welles was a very wise, strong man. There was nothing decorative about him; there was no noise in the street when he went along; but he understood his duty, and did it efficiently, continually, and unvaryingly. There was a good deal of opposition to him, for we had no navy when the war began, and he had to create one without much deliberation; but he was patient, laborious, and intelligent at his task.

Welles kept extensive diaries of his time in Lincoln's administration and they are fascinating. See Diary of Gideon Welles.—Ed. 2018

Montgomery Blair was Postmaster-General in Mr. Lincoln's Cabinet. He was a capable man, sharp, keen, perhaps a little cranky, and not friendly with everybody; but I always found him pleasant to deal with, and I saw a great deal of him. He and Mr. Stanton were not very good friends, and when he wanted anything in the War Department he was more likely to come to an old friend like me than to go to the Secretary. Stanton, too, rather preferred that.

The Attorney-General of the Cabinet was Edward Bates, of Missouri. Bates had been Mr. Greeley's favorite candidate for the presidency. He was put into the Cabinet partly, I suppose, because his reputation was good as a lawyer, but principally because he had been advocated for President by such powerful influences. Bates must have been about sixty-eight years old when he was appointed Attorney-General. He was a very eloquent speaker. Give him a patriotic subject, where his feelings could expand, and he would make a beautiful speech. He was a man of very gentle, cordial nature, but not one of extraordinary brilliancy.

The relations between Mr. Lincoln and the members of his Cabinet were always friendly and sincere on his part. He treated every one of them with unvarying candor, respect, and kindness; but, though several of them were men of extraordinary force and self-assertion—this was true especially of Mr. Seward, Mr. Chase, and Mr. Stanton—and though there was nothing of selfhood or domination in his manner toward them, it was always plain that he was the master and they the subordinates. They constantly had to yield to his will in questions where responsibility fell upon him. If he ever yielded to theirs, it was because they convinced him that the course they advised was judicious and appropriate. I fancied during the whole time of my intimate intercourse with him and with them that he was always prepared to receive the resignation of any one of them. At the same time I do not recollect a single occasion when any member of the Cabinet had got his mind ready to quit his post from any feeling of dissatisfaction with the policy or conduct of the President. Not that they were always satisfied with his actions; the members of the Cabinet, like human beings in general, were not pleased with everything. In their judgment much was imperfect in the administration; much, they felt, would have been done better if their views had been adopted and they individually had had charge of it. Not so with the President. He was calm, equable, uncomplaining. In the discussion of important questions, whatever he said showed the profoundest thought, even when he was joking. He seemed to see every side of every question. He never was impatient, he never was in a hurry, and he never tried to hurry anybody else. To everyone he was pleasant and cordial. Yet they all felt it was his word that went at last; that every case was open until he gave his decision.

This impression of authority, of reserve force, Mr. Lincoln always gave to those about him. Even physically he was impressive. According to the record measurements, he was six feet four inches in height. That is, he was at least four inches taller than the tall, ordinary man. When he rode out on horseback to review an army, as I have frequently seen him do, he wore usually a high hat, and then he looked like a giant. There was no waste or excess of material about his frame; nevertheless, he was very strong and muscular. I remember that the last time I went to see him at the White House—the afternoon before he was killed—I found him in a side room with coat off and sleeves rolled up, washing his hands. He had finished his work for the day, and was going away. I noticed then the thinness of his arms, and how well developed, strong, and active his muscles seemed to be. In fact, there was nothing flabby or feeble about Mr. Lincoln physically. He was a very quick man in his movements when he chose to be, and he had immense physical endurance. Night after night he would work late and hard without being wilted by it, and he always seemed as ready for the next day's work as though he had done nothing the day before.

Mr. Lincoln's face was thin, and his features were large. His hair was black, his eyebrows heavy, his forehead square and well developed. His complexion was dark and quite sallow. His smile was something most lovely. I have never seen a woman's smile that approached it in its engaging quality; nor have I ever seen another face which would light up as Mr. Lincoln's did when something touched his heart or amused him. I have heard it said that he was ungainly, that his step was awkward. He never impressed me as being awkward. In the first place, there was such a charm and beauty about his expression, such good humor and friendly spirit looking from his eyes, that when you were near him you never thought whether he was awkward or graceful; you thought of nothing except, What a kindly character this man has! Then, too, there was such shrewdness in his kindly features that one did not care to criticize him. His manner was always dignified, and even if he had done an awkward thing the dignity of his character and manner would have made it seem graceful and becoming.

The great quality of his appearance was benevolence and benignity: the wish to do somebody some good if he could; and yet there was no flabby philanthropy about Abraham Lincoln. He was all solid, hard, keen intelligence combined with goodness. Indeed, the expression of his face and of his bearing which impressed one most, after his benevolence and benignity, was his intelligent understanding. You felt that here was a man who saw through things, who understood, and you respected him accordingly.

Lincoln was a supreme politician. He understood politics because he understood human nature. I had an illustration of this in the spring of 1864. The administration had decided that the Constitution of the United States should be amended so that slavery should be prohibited. This was not only a change in our national policy, it was also a most important military measure. It was intended not merely as a means of abolishing slavery forever, but as a means of affecting the judgment and the feelings and the anticipations of those in rebellion. It was believed that such an amendment to the Constitution would be equivalent to new armies in the field, that it would be worth at least a million men, that it would be an intellectual army that would tend to paralyze the enemy and break the continuity of his ideas.

In order thus to amend the Constitution, it was necessary first to have the proposed amendment approved by three fourths of the States. When that question came to be considered, the issue was seen to be so close that one State more was necessary. The State of Nevada was organized and admitted into the Union to answer that purpose. I have sometimes heard people complain of Nevada as superfluous and petty, not big enough to be a State; but when I hear that complaint, I always hear Abraham Lincoln saying, "It is easier to admit Nevada than to raise another million of soldiers."

In March, 1864, the question of allowing Nevada to form a State government finally came up in the House of Representatives. There was strong opposition to it. For a long time beforehand the question had been canvassed anxiously. At last, late one afternoon, the President came into my office, in the third story of the War Department. He used to come there sometimes rather than send for me, because he was fond of walking and liked to get away from the crowds in the White House. He came in and shut the door.

"Dana," he said, "I am very anxious about this vote. It has got to be taken next week. The time is very short. It is going to be a great deal closer than I wish it was."

"There are plenty of Democrats who will vote for it," I replied. "There is James E. English, of Connecticut; I think he is sure, isn't he?"

"Oh, yes; he is sure on the merits of the question."

"Then," said I, "there's [Samuel] 'Sunset' Cox, of Ohio. How is he?"

"He is sure and fearless. But there are some others that I am not clear about. There are three that you can deal with better than anybody else, perhaps, as you know them all. I wish you would send for them."

He told me who they were; it isn't necessary to repeat the names here. One man was from New Jersey and two from New York.

"What will they be likely to want?" I asked.

"I don't know," said the President; "I don't know. It makes no difference, though, what they want. Here is the alternative: that we carry this vote, or be compelled to raise another million, and I don't know how many more, men, and fight no one knows how long. It is a question of three votes or new armies."

"Well, sir," said I, "what shall I say to these gentlemen?"

"I don't know," said he; "but whatever promise you make to them I will perform."

I sent for the men and saw them one by one. I found that they were afraid of their party. They said that some fellows in the party would be down on them. Two of them wanted internal revenue collector's appointments. "You shall have it," I said. Another one wanted a very important appointment about the custom house of New York. I knew the man well whom he wanted to have appointed. He was a Republican, though the congressman was a Democrat. I had served with him in the Republican county committee of New York. The office was worth perhaps twenty thousand dollars a year. When the congressman stated the case, I asked him, "Do you want that?"

"Yes," said he.

"Well," I answered, "you shall have it."

"I understand, of course," said he, "that you are not saying this on your own authority?"

"Oh, no," said I; "I am saying it on the authority of the President."

Well, these men voted that Nevada be allowed to form a State government, and thus they helped secure the vote which was required. The next October the President signed the proclamation admitting the State. In the February following Nevada was one of the States which ratified the Thirteenth Amendment, by which slavery was abolished by constitutional prohibition in all of the United States. I have always felt that this little piece of side politics was one of the most judicious, humane, and wise uses of executive authority that I have ever assisted in or witnessed.

The appointment in the New York Custom House was to wait until the term of the actual incumbent had run out. My friend, the Democratic congressman, was quite willing. "That's all right," he said; "I am in no hurry." Before the time had expired, Mr. Lincoln was murdered and Andrew Johnson became President. I was in the West, when one day I got a telegram from Roscoe Conkling:

"Come to Washington." So I went.

"I want you to go and see President Johnson," Mr. Conkling said, "and tell him that the appointment of this man to the custom house is a sacred promise of Mr. Lincoln's, and that it must be kept."

Then I went to the White House, and saw President Johnson.

"This is Mr. Lincoln's promise," I urged. "He regarded it as saving the necessity of another call for troops and raising, perhaps, a million more men to continue the war. I trust, Mr. President, that you will see your way clear to execute this promise."

"Well, Mr. Dana," he replied, "I don't say that I won't; but I have observed in the course of my experience that such bargains tend to immorality."

The appointment was not made. I am happy to say, however, that the gentleman to whom the promise was given never found any fault either with President Lincoln or with the Assistant Secretary who had been the means of making the promise to him.

One of the cleverest minor political moves which Mr. Lincoln ever made was an appointment he once gave Horace Greeley. Mr. Greeley never approved of Mr. Lincoln's manner of conducting the war, and he sometimes abused the President roundly for his deliberation. As the war went on, Greeley grew more and more irritable, because the administration did not make peace on some terms. Finally, in July, 1864, he received a letter from a pretended agent of the Confederate authorities in Canada, saying:

> I am authorized to state to you for our use only, not the public, that two ambassadors of Davis and Company are now in Canada with full and complete powers for a peace, and Mr. Sanders requests that you come on immediately to me at Cataract House to have a private interview; or, if you will send the President's protection for him and two friends, they will come on and meet you. He says the whole matter can be consummated by me, them, and President Lincoln.

This letter was followed the next day by a telegram, saying : "Will you come here? Parties have full power."

Upon receiving this letter, Mr. Greeley wrote to President Lincoln, more or less in the strain of the articles that he had published in the *Tribune*. He complained bitterly of the way the business of the Government was managed in the great crisis, and told the President that now there was a way open to peace. He explained that the Confederates wanted a conference, and he told Mr. Lincoln that he thought that he ought to appoint an ambassador, or a diplomatic agent, of the United States Government, to meet the Confederate agents at Niagara and hear what they had to say. Mr. Lincoln immediately responded by asking Mr. Greeley to be himself the representative and to go to Niagara Falls.

"If you can find any person anywhere," the President wrote, "professing to have any proposition of Jefferson Davis, in writing, for peace, embracing the restoration of the Union, and abandonment of slavery, whatever else it embraces, say to him he may come to me with you, and that if he really brings such proposition he shall at the least have safe conduct with the paper (and without publicity, if he chooses) to the point where you shall have met him. The same, if there be two or more persons."

Mr. Greeley went to Niagara, but his mission ended in nothing, except that the poor man, led astray by too great confidence, failed in his undertaking, and was almost universally laughed at. I saw the President not long after that, and he said, with a funny twinkle in his eye: "I sent Brother Greeley a commission. I guess I am about even with him now."

Lincoln had the most comprehensive, the most judicious mind; he was the least faulty in his conclusions of any man I have ever known. He never stepped too soon, and he never stepped too late. When the whole Northern country seemed to be clamoring for him to issue a proclamation abolishing slavery, he didn't do it. Deputation after deputation went to Washington. I remember once a hundred gentlemen, dressed in black coats, mostly clergymen, from Massachusetts, came to Washington to appeal to him to proclaim the abolition of slavery. But he did not do it. He allowed Mr. Cameron and General Butler to execute their great idea of treating slaves as contraband of war and protecting those who had got into our lines against being recaptured by their Southern owners; but he would not prematurely make the proclamation that was so much desired. Finally the time came, and of that he was the judge. Nobody else decided it; nobody commanded it; the proclamation was issued as he thought best, and it was efficacious. The people of the North, who during the long contest over slavery had always stood strenuously by the compromises of the Constitution, might themselves have become half rebels if this proclamation had been issued too soon. At last they were tired of waiting, tired of endeavoring to preserve even a show of regard for what was called "the compromises of the Constitution" when they believed the Constitution itself was in danger. Thus public opinion was ripe when the proclamation came, and that was the beginning of the end. He could have' issued this proclamation two years before, perhaps, and the consequence of it might have been our entire defeat; but when it came it did its work, and it did us no harm whatever. Nobody protested against it, not even the Confederates themselves.

This unerring judgment, this patience which waited and which knew when the right time had arrived, is an intellectual quality that I do not find exercised upon any such scale and with such absolute precision by any other man in history. It proves Abraham Lincoln to have been intellectually one of the greatest of rulers. If we look through the record of great men, where is there one to be placed beside him? I do not know.

Another interesting fact about Abraham Lincoln is that he developed into a great military man; that is to say, a man of supreme military judgment. I do not risk anything in saying that if one will study the records of the war and study the writings relating to it, he will agree with me that the greatest general we had, greater than Grant or Thomas, was Abraham Lincoln. It was not so at the beginning; but after three or four years of constant practice in the science and art of war, he arrived at this extraordinary knowledge of it, so that Von Moltke was not a better general, or an abler planner or expounder of a campaign, than was President Lincoln. To sum it up, he was a born leader of men. He knew human nature; he knew what chord to strike, and was never afraid to strike it when he believed that the time had arrived.

Mr. Lincoln was not what is called an educated man. In the college that he attended a man gets up at daylight to hoe corn, and sits up at night by the side of a burning pine-knot to read the best book he can find. What education he had, he had picked up. He had read a great many books, and all the books that he had read he knew. He had a tenacious memory, just as he had the ability to see the essential thing. He never took an unimportant point and went off upon that; but he always laid hold of the real question, and attended to that, giving no more thought to other points than was indispensably necessary.

Thus, while we say that Mr. Lincoln was an uneducated man in the college sense, he had a singularly perfect education in regard to everything that concerns the practical affairs of life. His judgment was excellent, and his information was always accurate. He knew what the thing was. He was a man of genius, and contrasted with men of education the man of genius will always carry the day. Many of his speeches illustrate this.

I remember very well Mr. Stanton's comment on the Gettysburg speeches of Edward Everett and Mr. Lincoln. "Edward Everett has made a speech [two hours long]," he said, "that will make three columns in the newspapers, and Mr. Lincoln has made a speech of perhaps forty or fifty lines [about two minutes long]. Everett's is the speech of a scholar, polished to the last possibility. It is elegant, and it is learned; but Lincoln's speech will be read by a thousand men where one reads Everett's, and will be remembered as long as anybody's speeches are remembered who speaks in the English language."

That was the truth. Whoever thinks of or reads Everett's Gettysburg speech now? If one will compare those two speeches he will get an idea how superior genius is to education; how superior that intellectual faculty is which sees the vitality of a question and knows how to state it; how superior that intellectual faculty is which regards everything with the fire of earnestness in the soul, with the relentless purpose of a heart devoted to objects beyond literature.

Another remarkable peculiarity of Mr. Lincoln's was that he seemed to have no illusions. He had no freakish notions that things were so, or might be so, when they were not so. All his thinking and reasoning, all his mind, in short, was based continually upon actual facts, and upon facts of which, as I said, he saw the essence. I never heard him say anything that was not so. I never heard him foretell things; he told what they were, but I never heard him intimate that such and such consequences were likely to happen without the consequences following. I should say, perhaps, that his greatest quality was wisdom. And that is something superior to talent, superior to education. It is again genius; I do not think it can be acquired. All the advice that he gave was wise, and it was always timely. This wisdom, it is scarcely necessary to add, had its animating philosophy in his own famous words, "With malice toward none, with charity for all."

Another remarkable quality of Mr. Lincoln was his great mercifulness. A thing it seemed as if he could not do was to sign a death warrant. One day General Augur, who was the major general commanding the forces in and around Washington, came to my office and said:

"Here is So-and-So, a spy. He has been tried by court-martial; the facts are perfectly established, he has been sentenced to death, and here is the warrant for his execution, which is fixed for tomorrow morning at six o'clock. The President is away. If he were here, the man certainly wouldn't be executed. He isn't here. I think it very essential to the safety of the service and the safety of everything that an example should be made of this spy. They do us great mischief; and it is very important that the law which all nations recognize in dealing with spies, and the punishment which every nation assigns to them, should be inflicted upon at least one of these wretches who haunt us around Washington. Do you know whether the President will be back before morning?"

"I understand that he won't be back until tomorrow afternoon," I replied.

"Well, as the President is not here, will you sign the warrant?"

"Go to Mr. Stanton," I said; "he is the authority."

"I have been to him, and he said I should come to you."

Well, I signed the order; I agreed with General Augur in his view of the question. At about eleven o'clock the next day I met the general. "The President got home at two o'clock this morning," he said, "and he stopped it all."

But it was not only in matters of life and death that Mr. Lincoln was merciful. He was kind at heart toward all the world. I never heard him say an unkind thing about anybody. Now and then he would laugh at something jocose or satirical that somebody had done or said, but it was always pleasant humor. He would never allow the wants of any man or woman to go unattended to if he could help it. I noticed his sweetness of nature particularly with his little son, a child at that time perhaps seven or nine years old, who used to roam the departments and whom everybody called "Tad." He had a defective palate, and couldn't speak very plainly. Often I have sat by his father, reporting to him some important matter that I had been ordered to inquire into, and he would have this boy on his knee. While he would perfectly understand the report, the striking thing about him was his affection for the child.

He was good to everybody. Once there was a great gathering at the White House on New Year's Day, and all the diplomats came in their uniforms, and all the officers of the army and navy in Washington were in full costume. A little girl of mine said, "Papa, couldn't you take me over to see that?" I said, "Yes so I took her over and put her in a corner, where she beheld this gorgeous show. When it was finished, I went up to Mr. Lincoln and said, "I have a little girl here who wants to shake hands with you." He went over to her, and took her up and kissed her and talked to her. She will never forget it if she lives to be a thousand years old.

THE ARMY OF THE POTOMAC IN '64

I remained in Washington the entire winter of 1863-64, occupied mainly with the routine business of the department. Meantime the Chattanooga victory had made Grant the great military figure of the country, and deservedly so. The grade of lieutenant general had been immediately revived by act of Congress, and the President had promptly promoted him to the new rank, and made him general in chief of all the armies of the United States. His military prestige was such that everything was put into his hands, everything yielded to his wishes. The coming of Grant was a great relief to the President and the Secretary. Halleck, the late general in chief, consented to serve as Grant's chief of staff in Washington, practically continuing his old service of chief military adviser to the President and the Secretary of War, while Grant took the field in active direction of operations against Richmond.

Halleck was not thought to be a great man in the field, but he was nevertheless a man of military ability, and by reason of his great accomplishments in the technics of armies and of war was almost invaluable as an adviser to the civilians Lincoln and Stanton. He was an honest man, perhaps somewhat lacking in moral courage, yet earnest and energetic in his efforts to sustain the national government. I have heard Halleck accused of being unjust to his inferiors in rank, especially to Grant. I believe this wrong. I never thought him unjust to anybody. He always had his own ideas, and insisted strenuously on following his own course, but I never detected a sign of injustice in his conduct toward others. I think this false impression came from the fact that he was a very critical man. The first impulse of his mind toward a new plan was not enthusiasm; it was analysis, criticism. His habit of picking men and manners to pieces to see what they were worth gave the idea that he was unjust and malicious toward certain of his subordinates.

It was March when Grant came to Washington to receive his new grade of lieutenant general. Soon afterward he joined the

Army of the Potomac. On the 4th of May he had moved out from Culpeper, where the army had been in winter quarters since the previous December, and crossed the Rapidan with an effective force of one hundred and twenty thousand men. General Lee, his opponent, had about seventy thousand.

For two days after Grant moved we had no authentic reports from the army, although it was known that great events were occurring. Mr. Stanton and Mr. Lincoln had begun to get uneasy. The evening of May 6th I was at a reception when a messenger came with summons to the War Department. I hurried over to the office in evening dress. The President was there, talking very soberly with Stanton.

"Dana," said Mr. Lincoln, "you know we have been in the dark for two days since Grant moved. We are very much troubled, and have concluded to send you down there. How soon can you start?"

"In half an hour," I replied.

In about that time I had an engine fired up at Alexandria, and a cavalry escort of a hundred men awaiting me there. I had got into my camp clothes, had borrowed a pistol, and with my own horse was aboard the train at Maryland Avenue that was to take me to Alexandria. My only baggage was a toothbrush. I was just starting when an orderly galloped up with word that the President wished to see me. I rode back to the department in hot haste. Mr. Lincoln was sitting in the same place.

"Well, Dana," said he, looking up, "since you went away I've been thinking about it. I don't like to send you down there."

"But why not, Mr. President?" I asked, a little surprised.

"You can't tell," continued the President, "just where Lee is or what he is doing, and Jeb Stuart is rampaging around pretty lively in between the Rappahannock and the Rapidan. It's a considerable risk, and I don't like to expose you to it."

"Mr. President," I said, "I have a cavalry guard ready and a good horse myself. If we are attacked, we probably will be strong enough to fight. If we are not strong enough to fight, and it comes to the worst, we are equipped to run. It's getting late, and I want to get down to the Rappahannock by daylight. I think I'll start."

"Well, now, Dana," said the President, with a little twinkle in his eyes, "if you feel that way, I rather wish you would. Good night, and God bless you."

By seven o'clock on the morning of May 7th I was at the Rappahannock, where I found a rear guard of the army. I stopped there for breakfast, and then hurried on to Grant's headquarters, which were at Piney Branch Meeting House. There I learned of the crossing of the Rapidan by our army, and of the desperate battle of the Wilderness on May 5th and 6th.

The Army of the Potomac was then composed of the Second, Fifth, Sixth, and Ninth Army Corps, and of one cavalry corps. In command of the army was Major-General George C. Meade. He was a tall, thin man, rather dyspeptic, I should suppose from the fits of nervous irritation to which he was subject. He was totally lacking in cordiality toward those with whom he had business, and in consequence was generally disliked by his subordinates. With General Grant Meade got along always perfectly, because he had the first virtue of a soldier—that is, obedience to orders. He was an intellectual man, and agreeable to talk with when his mind was free, but silent and indifferent to everybody when he was occupied, with that which interested him.

As a commander, Meade seemed to me to lack the boldness that was necessary to bring the war to a close. He lacked self-confidence and tenacity of purpose, and he had not the moral authority that Grant had attained from his grand successes in other fields. As soon as Meade had a commander over him he was all right, but when he himself was the commander he began to hesitate. Meade had entirely separate headquarters and a separate staff, and Grant sent his orders to him.

In command of the Second Army Corps was Major-General [Winfield Scott] Hancock. He was a splendid fellow, a brilliant man, as brave as Julius Caesar, and always ready to obey orders, especially if they were fighting orders. He had more of the aggressive spirit than almost anybody else in that army. Major-General [Gouverneur Kemble] Warren, who commanded the Fifth Army Corps, was an accomplished engineer. Major-General John Sedgwick commanded the Sixth Army Corps. I had known him for over twenty years. Sedgwick graduated at West Point in 1837, and was appointed a second lieutenant in the Second Artillery. At the time of the McKenzie rebellion in Canada Sedgwick's company was stationed at Buffalo during a considerable time. I was living in Buffalo then, and in this rebellion the young men of the town organized a regiment of city guards, and I was a sergeant in one of those companies, so that I became quite familiar with all the military movements then going on. Then it was that I got acquainted with Sedgwick. He was a very solid man; no flummery about him. You could always tell where Sedgwick was to be found, and in a battle he was apt to be found where the hardest fighting was. He was not an ardent, impetuous soldier like Hancock, but was steady and sure.

Two days after I reached the army, on May 9th, not far from Spottsylvania Courthouse, my old friend Sedgwick was killed. He had gone out in the morning to inspect his lines, and, getting beyond the point of safety, was struck in the forehead by a sharpshooter and instantly killed.

Reportedly Sedgwick was striding in front of his lines and his last words were, "What? Men dodging this way for single bullets? What will you do when they open fire along the whole line? "Why are you dodging like this? They couldn't hit an elephant at this distance."—Ed. 2018

The command of the Sixth Army Corps was given to General H. G. Wright. Wright was another engineer officer, well educated, of good, solid intellect, with capacity for command, but no special predilection for fighting. From the moment Meade assumed command of the army, two days before Gettysburg, the engineers rapidly came to the front, for Meade had the pride of corps strongly implanted in his heart.

Major-General Burnside, whom I had last seen at Knoxville in December, was in command of the Ninth Army Corps. Immediately after the siege of Knoxville, at his own request, Burnside had been relieved of the command in East Tennessee by Major-General John G. Foster. The President somehow always showed for Burnside great respect and good will. After Grant's plans for the spring campaign were made known, the Ninth Corps was moved by rail to Annapolis, where it was recruited up to about twenty-five thousand men. As the time for action neared it was set in motion, and by easy marches reached and re-enforced the Army of the Potomac on the morning of the 6th of May, in the midst of the battle of the Wilderness. It was not formally incorporated with that army until later, but, by a sort of fiction, it was held to be a distinct army, Burnside acting in concert with Meade, and receiving his orders directly from Grant, as did Meade. These two armies were the excuse for Grant's personal presence, without actually superseding Meade.

In my opinion, the great soldier of the Army of the Potomac at this time was General Humphreys.

Andrew Atkinson Humphreys (1810 – 1883) wrote a memoir of the last year of the war, which was very well received by his former colleagues in arms. See [The Virginia Campaign: Last year of the Civil War](#)*.—Ed. 2018*

He was the chief of staff to General Meade, and was a strategist, a tactician, and an engineer. Humphreys was a fighter, too, and in this an exception to most engineers. He was a very interesting figure. He used to ride about in a black felt hat, the brim of which was turned down all around, making him look like a Quaker. He was very pleasant to deal with, unless you were fighting against him, and then he was not so pleasant. He was one of the loudest swearers that I ever knew. The men of distinguished and brilliant profanity in the war were General Sherman and General Humphreys—I could not mention any others that could be classed with them. General Logan also was a strong swearer, but he was not a West Pointer: he was a civilian. Sherman and Humphreys would swear to make everything blue when some dispatch had not been delivered correctly or they were provoked. Humphreys was a very charming man, quite destitute of vanity. I think he had consented to go and serve with Meade as chief of staff out of pure patriotism. He preferred an active command, and eventually, on the eve of the end, succeeded to the command of the Second Corps, and bore a conspicuous part in the Appomattox campaign.

Meade was in command of the Army of the Potomac, but it was Grant, the lieutenant general of the armies of the United States, who was really directing the movements. The central idea of the campaign had not developed to the army when I reached headquarters, but it was soon clear to everybody. Grant's great operation was the endeavor to interpose the Federal army between Lee's army and Richmond, so as to cut Lee off from his base of supplies. He meant to get considerably in advance of Lee—between him and Richmond—thus compelling Lee to leave his entrenchments and hasten southward. If in the collision thus forced Grant found that he could not smash Lee, he meant to make another move to get behind his army. That was to be the strategy of the campaign of 1864. That was what Lee thwarted, though he had a narrow escape more than once.

The first encounter with Lee had taken place in the Wilderness on May 5th and 6th. The Confederates and many Northern writers love to call the Wilderness a drawn battle. It was not so; in every essential light it was a Union victory. Grant had not intended to fight a battle in those dense, brushy jungles, but Lee precipitated it just as he had precipitated the battle of Chancellorsville one year before, and not six miles to the eastward of this very ground. In doing so he hoped to neutralize the superior numbers of Grant as he had Hooker's, and so to mystify and handle the Union leader as to compel a retreat across the Rapidan. But he failed. Some of the fighting in the brush was a draw, but the Union army did not yield a rood of ground; it held the roads southward, inflicted great losses on its enemy, and then, instead of recrossing the river, resumed its march toward Richmond as soon as Lee's attacks had ceased. Lee had palpably failed in his objects. His old-time tactics had made no impression on Grant. He never offered general battle in the open afterward.

The previous history of the Army of the Potomac had been to advance and fight a battle, then either to retreat or to lie still, and finally to go into winter quarters. Grant did not intend to proceed in that way. As soon as he had fought a battle and had not routed Lee, he meant to move nearer to Richmond and fight another battle. But the men in the army had become so accustomed to the old methods of campaigning that few, if any, of them believed that the new commander in chief would be able to do differently from his predecessors. I remember distinctly the sensation in the ranks when the rumor first went around that our position was south of Lee's. It was the morning of May 8th. The night before the army had made a forced march on Spottsylvania Courthouse. There was no indication the next morning that Lee had moved in any direction. As the army began to realize that we were really moving south, and at that moment were probably much nearer Richmond than was our enemy, the spirits of men and officers rose to the highest pitch of animation. On every hand I heard the cry, "On to Richmond!"

But there were to be a great many more obstacles to our reaching Richmond than General Grant himself, I presume, realized on May 8, 1864. We met one that very morning; for when our advance reached Spottsylvania Courthouse it found Lee's troops there, ready to dispute the right of way with us, and two days later Grant was obliged to fight the battle of Spottsylvania before we could make another move south.

It is no part of my present plan to go into detailed description of all the battles of this campaign, but rather to dwell on the incidents and deeds which impressed me most deeply at the moment. In the battle of Spottsylvania, a terrific struggle, with many dramatic features, there is nothing I remember more distinctly than a little scene in General Grant's tent between him and a captured Confederate officer, General Edward Johnson. The battle had begun on the morning of May 10th, and had continued all day. On the 11th the armies had rested, but at half past four on the morning of the 12th fighting had been begun by an attack by Hancock on a rebel salient. Hancock attacked with his accustomed impetuosity, storming and capturing the enemy's fortified line, with some four thousand prisoners and twenty cannon. The captures included nearly all of Major-General Edward Johnson's division, together with Johnson himself and General George H. Steuart.

I was at Grant's headquarters when General Johnson was brought in a prisoner. He was a West Pointer, and had been a captain in the old army before secession, and was an important officer in the Confederate service, having distinguished himself in the Valley in 1863, and at Gettysburg. Grant had not seen him since they had been in Mexico together. The two men shook hands cordially, and at once began a brisk conversation, which was very interesting to me, because nothing was said in it on the subject in which they were both most interested just then—that is, the fight that was going on, and the surprise that Hancock had effected. It was the past alone of which they talked.

It was quite early in the morning when Hancock's prisoners were brought in. The battle raged without cessation throughout the day, Wright and Hancock bearing the brunt of it. Burnside made several attacks, in which his troops generally bore themselves like good soldiers. The results of the battle of Spottsylvania were that we had crowded the enemy out of some of his most important positions, had weakened him by losses of between nine thousand and ten thousand men killed, wounded, and captured, besides many battle flags and much artillery, and that our troops rested victorious upon the ground they had fought for.

After the battle was over and firing had nearly ceased, Rawlins and I went out to ride over the field. We went first to the salient which Hancock had attacked in the morning. The two armies had struggled for hours for this point, and the loss had been so terrific that the place has always been known since as the "Bloody Angle." The ground around the salient had been trampled and cut in the struggle until it was almost impassable for one on horseback, so

Rawlins and I dismounted and climbed up the bank over the outer line of the rude breastworks. Within we saw a fence over which earth evidently had been banked, but which now was bare and half down. It was here the fighting had been fiercest. We picked our way to this fence, and stopped to look over the scene. The night was coming on, and, after the horrible din of the day, the silence was intense; nothing broke it but distant and occasional firing or the low groans of the wounded. I remember that as I stood there I was almost startled to hear a bird twittering in a tree. All around us the underbrush and trees, which were just beginning to be green, had been riddled and burnt. The ground was thick with dead and wounded men, among whom the relief corps was at work. The earth, which was soft from the heavy rains we had been having before and during the battle, had been trampled by the fighting of the thousands of men until it was soft, like thin hasty pudding. Over the fence against which we leaned lay a great pool of this mud, its surface as smooth as that of a pond.

As we stood there, looking silently down at it, of a sudden the leg of a man was lifted up from the pool and the mud dripped off his boot. It was so unexpected, so horrible, that for a moment we were stunned. Then we pulled ourselves together and called to some soldiers nearby to rescue the owner of the leg. They pulled him out with but little trouble, and discovered that he was not dead, only wounded. He was taken to the hospital, where he got well, I believe.

The first news which passed through the ranks the morning after the battle of Spottsylvania was that Lee had abandoned his position during the night. Though our army was greatly fatigued from the enormous efforts of the day before, the news of Lee's departure inspired the men with fresh energy, and everybody was eager to be in pursuit. Our skirmishers soon found the enemy along the whole line, however, and the conclusion was that their retrograde movement had been made to correct their position after the loss of the key points taken from them the day before, and that they were still with us in a new line as strong as the old one. Of course, we could not determine this point without a battle, and nothing was done that day to provoke one. It was necessary to rest the men.

In changing his lines Lee had left more uncovered the roads leading southward along his right wing, and Grant ordered Meade to throw the corps of Warren, which held the right, and the corps of Wright, which held the center of Meade's army, to the left of Burnside, leaving Hancock upon our right. If not interrupted, Grant thought by this maneuver to turn Lee's flank and compel him to move southward.

The movement of the two corps to our left was executed during the night of May 13th and 14th, but for three days it had rained steadily, and the roads were so bad that Wright and Warren did not get up to surprise the enemy at daylight as ordered. The only engagement brought on by this move was an active little fight over a conspicuous hill, with a house and plantation buildings upon it. The hill, which was on our left and the enemy's right, was valuable as a lookout rather than for offensive operations. Upton took it in the morning, and later the enemy retook it. General Meade, who was there at that moment, narrowly escaped capture. Our men very handsomely carried the hill again that evening.

The two armies were then lying in a semicircle, the Federal left well around toward the south. We were concentrated to the last degree, and, so far as we could tell, Lee's forces were equally compact. On the 15th, 16th, and 17th, we lay in about the same position. This inactivity was caused by the weather. A pouring rain had begun on the 11th, and it continued until the morning of the 16th; the mud was so deep that any offensive operation, however successful, could not be followed up. There was nothing to do but lie still and wait for better weather and drier roads.

While waiting for the rain to stop, we had time to consider the field returns of losses as they were handed in. The army had left winter quarters at Culpeper Courthouse on May 4th, and on May 16th the total of killed, wounded, and missing in both the Army of the Potomac and the Ninth Corps amounted to a little over thirty-three thousand men. The missing alone amounted to forty-nine hundred, but some of these were, in fact, killed or wounded. When Grant looked over the returns, he expressed great regret at the loss of so many men. Meade, who was with him, remarked, as I remember, "Well, General, we can't do these little tricks without losses."

THE GREAT GAME BETWEEN GRANT AND LEE

By the afternoon of May 17th the weather was splendid, and the roads were rapidly becoming dry, even where the mud was worst. Grant determined to engage Lee, and orders for a decisive movement of the army were issued, to be executed during the night. At first he proposed an attack upon the enemy's right, but changed the plan. Instead of attacking there, Hancock and Wright made a night march back to our right flank, and attacked at daylight upon the same lines where Hancock made his successful assault on the 12th. They succeeded in pressing close to the enemy's lines, and for a time were confident that at last they had struck the lair of the enemy, but an impassable abatis stopped them. One division of Hancock's corps attempted in vain to charge through this obstacle, and held the ground before it for an hour or more under a galling fire of canister. The difficulty of storming the enemy's entrenched camp on that side being evidently of the most extreme character, and both corps having artfully but unsuccessfully sought for a weak point where they might break through, Grant, at nine o'clock, ordered the attack to cease. The attempt was a failure. Lee was not to be ousted; and Grant, convinced of it, issued orders for another movement which he had had in contemplation for several days, but which he did not wish to try till after a last attempt to get the enemy out of his stronghold. This was nothing less than to slip away from Lee and march on toward Richmond again.

The new order directed that Hancock's corps should march by night from its present position southeast as far toward Richmond on the line of the Fredericksburg road as he could go, fighting his way if necessary. Warren was to follow, and, if Lee did not come out and attack when our army was thus weakened, Wright and Burnside also were to march southward.

This movement was begun on the night of the 20th. By the night of the 21st Hancock was across the Mattapony River at Milford. Warren had crossed the same river at Guiney's Station, the point to which Grant had moved his headquarters. By the morning of the 22d Wright and Burnside were up in safety, and the forward movement was continued. We were now in a fine, clear country, good to move in and fight in, and the advance of the 22d was most successful. By night our army lay in an east and west line along the Mattapony River, holding the crossings. On the right was Wright; close to him at the left, Warren; in the center, Burnside; on the left, Hancock. Our headquarters were at New Bethel Church. Our talk that night was that in all probability we should meet the enemy on the North Anna, a day's march to the south of our position.

The operations of the next day were much embarrassed by our ignorance of the road and the entire incorrectness of our maps; nevertheless, by one o'clock in the afternoon our right wing, under Warren, reached the North Anna. The stream there was about one hundred and fifty feet wide, with bluff banks from fifty to seventy-five feet high. Wright followed after Warren. As soon as Warren reached Jericho Mills he pushed his sharpshooters across the stream, which was easily fordable at that place, following them with a compact body of infantry. A Confederate regiment posted to watch the crossing at once gave way, leaving a single prisoner in our hands. From this man Warren learned that another of the enemy's divisions was drawn up to receive him nearby. Under the orders of General Grant, he promptly threw across the pontoon bridge, over which he rapidly moved his artillery, at the same time urging forward his infantry by the ford as well as by the bridge; and by five o'clock he had transported his entire command, and had taken up a position of great strength. Here he rapidly commenced entrenching himself.

Grant had by this time moved his headquarters up to Mount Carmel Church, some four miles from Jericho Mills. About six o'clock we knew from the firing that Warren had been attacked. I never heard more rapid or heavier firing, either of artillery or musketry. It was not until about half past ten that evening that we knew surely how the fight had gone; then a dispatch from Warren announced that he had triumphantly repulsed the enemy, and made considerable captures of prisoners.

About the same time that Warren was fighting for his position at Jericho Mills, Hancock advanced on our left. By a vigorous charge of two brigades of Birney's division, the enemy was driven over the North Anna River. The next morning Hancock crossed over. That same morning, May 24th, we found that, as a result of the operations of the previous day, we had about one thousand prisoners. They were more discouraged than any set of prisoners I ever saw before. Lee had deceived them, they said, and they declared that his army would not fight again except behind breastworks.

The general opinion of every prominent officer in the army on the morning of the 24th was that the enemy had fallen back, either to take up a position beyond the South Anna or to go to Richmond, but by noon the next day we knew this was a mistake. All through the day of the 24th Lee blocked our southward march. The opinion prevailed that the enemy's position was held by a rear guard only, but the Obstinacy of their skirmishers was regarded as very remarkable. About dark Hancock made an attack, breaking into the Confederate line of works, taking some prisoners, and satisfying himself that a whole corps was before him. Soon afterward the division of Gibbon was attacked, but it beat back the assault handsomely without any considerable loss. Just before dark Crittenden—the same Crittenden who was at Chickamauga—was also suddenly attacked, and one of his brigades damaged. No fighting of any moment took place on the morning of the 25th, but the enemy showed such strength as to leave no doubt that Lee's whole army was present. His entrenchments were in the form of the letter V. He showed artillery on both faces. By the morning of the 25th Grant was sure that Lee was before him and strongly entrenched. He soon determined on a new move. This was to withdraw his whole army as quickly as possible, and, before Lee discovered his intention, to move it southeast, across the Pamunkey, and perhaps on across the Chickahominy and the James, if he could not meanwhile get Lee out of his earthworks.

The orders for the new move were received with the best spirit by the army, in spite of the fact that the men were much jaded. Indeed, one of the most important results of the campaign thus far was the entire change which had taken place in the feelings of the armies. The Confederates had lost all confidence, and were already morally defeated. Our army had learned to believe that it was sure of ultimate victory. Even our officers had ceased to regard Lee as an invincible military genius. On the part of the enemy this change was evinced not only by their not attacking, even when circumstances seemed to invite it, but by the unanimous statements of prisoners taken from them.

The morning after we began to move from our position on the North Anna I was so confident that I wrote Mr. Stanton, "Rely upon it, the end is near as well as sure."

It was on the night of the 26th that our army was withdrawn from the North Anna, without loss or disturbance, and by the evening of the 27th Grant had his headquarters ten miles from Hanovertown, and his whole army was well up toward the crossing. We had no news of Lee's movements that day, though we heard that there was a force of the enemy at Hanover Courthouse. Grant himself was very doubtful that day of our getting across the Hanover Ferry; he told me that we might be obliged to go farther to the southeast to get over. On the morning of the 27th Sheridan and his cavalry seized the ferry, laying bridges, and, after crossing, advancing well beyond. Everything went on finely that night and during the 28th, the troops passing our headquarters in great numbers and very rapidly. By noon of the 28th the movement of the army across the Pamunkey was complete, with the exception of Burnside, who did not arrive until midnight. The movement had been executed with admirable celerity and success. The new position was one of great strength, our lines extending from the Pamunkey to Totopotomoy Creek. Wright was on the Pamunkey, Hancock on his left, and Warren on the Totopotomoy. The orders for that day were to let the men rest, though both officers and men were in high spirits at the successful execution of this long and difficult flank movement.

We were now south of the Pamunkey, and occupying a very strong position, but we did not know yet where Lee was. A general reconnaissance was at once ordered, and the enemy was found in force south of the Totopotomoy Creek; by the 30th there was no doubt that Lee's whole army, now re-enforced by thirteen thousand men, was close at hand and strongly entrenched again. Grant said he would fight here if there was a fair chance, but he declared emphatically he would not run his head against heavy works.

Our line began to push forward on the 30th. All the afternoon of that day at headquarters, which were now at Hawes's Shop, we heard the noise of fighting. First Warren on the left, who had reached a point only about seven miles and a half from Richmond, had a short, sharp, and decisive engagement with Early; and later an active conflict raged for some time with our right on the Totopotomoy. We were successful all along the line. The next day, the 31st, we pushed ahead until our lines lay from Bethesda Church, on the east, to the railroad, on the west. Desultory firing was constantly heard, but there was no very active fighting that day until about five o'clock in the afternoon, when Sheridan's cavalry, by hard work, drove out the enemy and secured Cold Harbor, which was at that moment of vast importance to us strategically.

It was determined to make a fight here before the enemy could entrench. Wright was at once ordered to have his whole force on the ground by daylight on the 1st of June, to support Sheridan and take the offensive. [William Farrar] "Baldy" Smith, of Butler's army, who had landed at White House on the 31st with twelve thousand five hundred men, was ordered to the aid of Wright and Sheridan. But there was an error in Smith's orders, and Wright's march was so long that his corps did not get up to Cold Harbor until the afternoon of the 1st. Meanwhile Sheridan's cavalry had repulsed two attacks by two brigades of Kershaw's infantry.

It was not until six o'clock in the afternoon that we at headquarters at Bethesda Church heard the cannon which indicated that an attack had at last been made by Wright and

Smith. From the sounds of artillery and musketry, we judged the fight was furious. Rickett's division broke through the rebel lines between Hoke and Kershaw, capturing five hundred prisoners, and forcing the enemy to take up a new position farther back. Smith's troops effected lodgments close up to the Confederate entrenchments. Our losses this day were twenty-two hundred men in these two corps. Warren was slightly engaged. Altogether they had done very well, but meanwhile Lee was again concentrated and entrenched in our front.

Hancock was ordered to move during the night, and his advance arrived at Cold Harbor about daylight. When I got up in the morning—I was then at Bethesda Church—his rear was marching past our headquarters. In conjunction with Wright and Smith, he was to fall upon Lee's right that day. Warren and Burnside were also ordered in as soon as they heard that the three corps on our left had begun battle. There was no battle that day, however. Hancock's men were so tired with their forced march of nearly twelve miles, and the heat and dust were so oppressive, that General Grant ordered the attack to be postponed until half past four o'clock the next morning.

So the battle Grant sought did not come until June 3d—that of Cold Harbor. On the morning of the 3d our line lay with the right at Bethesda Church, the left extending to the Chickahominy. Hancock commanded the left; next to him was Wright, with his corps drawn up in three lines; next, Smith, with the Eighteenth Corps in two lines; next, Warren, who had his whole command in a single line, the distance he covered being fully three miles. With this thin order of battle he was necessarily unable to make any effective assault. Burnside held the extreme right. Hancock, Wright, and Smith were to make the main attacks at daybreak. Promptly at the hour they dashed out toward the rebel lines, under a fearful fire of musketry and a cross fire of artillery. The losses were great, but we gained advantages here and there. The entire charge consumed hardly more than an hour. Barlow, of Hancock's corps, drove through a very strong line, and at five o'clock reported that he had taken entrenchments with guns and colors, but he could not stay there. An interior breastwork commanded the one he had carried, and his men had to withdraw, leaving behind them the captured cannon, and bringing out a single Confederate standard and two hundred and twenty prisoners as tokens of their brief success. Wright and Smith succeeded in carrying the first line of rifle-pits, but could get no farther to the front. All our forces held ground close up to the enemy. At some points they were entrenched within a hundred feet of the rebel breastworks. Burnside, on the right, captured some rifle-pits. Later he was attacked by Early, who was roughly handled and repulsed.

Warren was active, and repulsed a vigorous attack by Gordon.

Thus by noon we had fully developed the Confederate lines, and Grant could see what was necessary in order to get through them. Hancock reported that in his front it could not be done. Wright was decidedly of the opinion that a lodgment could be made in his front, but it would be difficult to make much by it unless Hancock and Smith could also advance. Smith thought he could carry the works before him, but was not sanguine. Burnside also thought he could get through, but Warren, who was nearest him, did not seem to share his opinion. In this state of things, at half past one o'clock, General Grant ordered the attack to be suspended. He had told Meade as early as seven in the morning to suspend the movement if it became evident that success was impossible.

This was the battle of Cold Harbor, which has been exaggerated into one of the bloodiest disasters of history, a reckless, useless waste of human life. It was nothing of the kind. The outlook warranted the effort. The breaking of Lee's lines meant his destruction and the collapse of the rebellion. Sheridan took the same chances at Five Forks ten months later, and won; so did Wright, Humphreys, [John] Gibbon, and others at Petersburg. They broke through far stronger lines than those at Cold Harbor, and Lee fled in the night toward Appomattox. So it would have been at Cold Harbor if Grant had won, and who would have thought of the losses?

While we lay at Cold Harbor, as when we had been at Spottsylvania, the principal topic of conversation was the losses of the army. The discussion has never ceased. There are still many persons who bitterly accuse Grant of butchery in this campaign. As a matter of fact, Grant lost fewer men in his successful effort to take Richmond and end the war than his predecessors lost in making the same attempt and failing. Grant in eleven months secured the prize with less loss than his predecessors suffered in failing to win it during a struggle of three years.

THE MARCH ON PETERSBURG

The affair of June 3d at Cold Harbor showed that Lee was not to be driven from his position without a great sacrifice of life. A left flank movement south of the James River was accordingly decided upon by Grant. This was no new idea; that eventuality had been part of the original plan of campaign, and preparations for bridging the James had been ordered as early as the 15th of April, three weeks before the battle of the Wilderness. One object of the movement across the James was to cut off Richmond's line of supplies from the south. But before this could be done another matter had to be attended to.

In General Grant's plan of campaign the effectual destruction of the Virginia Central Railroad was an indispensable feature. In moving from Culpeper he had expected that before reaching the Chickahominy he would have a chance to crush Lee's army by fighting. This would have allowed him an undisturbed opportunity to destroy that road, as well as the Fredericksburg road from the Chickahominy to the North Anna. The expectation had been disappointed by Lee's success in avoiding a decisive battle. Before moving farther in accomplishing the great object of the campaign, these roads must be so thoroughly destroyed that when Richmond was cut off from other lines of communication with the south the attempt to repair and use the line through Gordonsville and Lynchburg would be hopeless. The work was first to be attempted by Sheridan with cavalry. If he was not able to complete it, the whole army was to be swung around for the purpose, even should it be necessary to abandon temporarily our communications with White House.

This necessity, as well as that of making thorough preparations for the difficult march south of the James and for the perfect co-operation of Butler at Bermuda Hundred, detained Grant at Cold Harbor until June 12th. Two officers of his staff, Colonel Comstock and Colonel Porter, had been sent to General Butler to arrange for co-operation in the movement of the army to Bermuda Hundred, and to look over the ground to be traversed and the means of crossing the river. Grant would not order the movement until they returned. They did not get back until the 12th.

During this time the opposing lines of Grant and Lee were very close together, and on our side the troops made regular siege approaches to the Confederate works. The days passed quietly, with no fighting except an occasional rattle of musketry and now and then a cannon shot. There was occasionally a scare on the line. On the evening of June 5th Wright's and Hancock's line responded to a stiff assault; the firing lasted for twenty minutes, and it was very loud, but it was all about nothing and no harm was done. The enemy were so near that in the dark our men thought they were coming out to attack. On June 6th there was an onslaught on Burnside just after midnight, which was successfully repulsed, and in the afternoon a rush was made by a party of a hundred picked men of the enemy, who came to find out what was the meaning of Hancock's advancing siege lines. As a rule, everything was quiet except the picket firing, which could not be prevented when the men were so close together. The picket firing ceased only during the occasional truces to bury the dead.

The operations around Cold Harbor, the close proximity of the two lines, the unceasing firing, with no hour in the day or night when one could not hear the sound of musketry and cannon, were precisely like the conditions at Spottsylvania and those on the North Anna. It was a constant feeling for the weak spot in Lee's armor. There was far less maneuvering at Cold Harbor after the first efforts than during the long struggle at Spottsylvania. We were merely waiting for the proper moment to withdraw toward the James. Grant, Meade, and all the leading officers were certain of ultimate success; although the fighting had been more severe and continuous than anything in the previous history of the army, I must say a cheerful, confident tone generally prevailed. All acted as if they were at a job which required only time to finish.

Grant was disappointed, and talked to me a good deal about the failure to get at Lee in an open battle which would wind up the Confederacy. The general was constantly revolving plans to turn

Lee out of his entrenchments. The old-time fear of Lee's superior ability that was rife among the officers of the Army of the Potomac had entirely disappeared. They had begun to look upon him as an ordinary mortal, making a fairly good effort to ward off fate, and nothing more. I think Grant respected Lee's military ability and character, yet the boldness with which he maneuvered in Lee's presence is proof that he was not overawed by Lee's prestige as a strategist and tactician. He thought Lee's great forte was as a defensive fighter, a quality displayed at Antietam and Fredericksburg; but held no high opinion of his Chancellorsville operations, where he had recklessly laid himself open to ruin. To me the views of the military men at the different headquarters were interesting and instructive.

While on his round-the-world tour, post-presidency, Grant told newspaperman John Russell Young that he did not share other generals' exalted opinion of Lee and that he never felt as much anxiety facing Lee as he did Joe Johnston.—Ed. 2018

While we were encamped at Cold Harbor, General Meade was very much disturbed by a letter published in a Cincinnati paper, saying that after the battle of the Wilderness he counselled retreat—a course which would have destroyed the nation, but which Grant prohibited. This was entirely untrue. Meade had not shown any weakness since moving from Culpeper, nor once intimated doubt as to the successful issue of the campaign. Nor had he intimated that any other plan or line would be more likely to win. The newspaper correspondent who was responsible for the misstatement was with us, and Meade ordered that, as a punishment, he should be paraded through the lines and afterward expelled from the army. This was done on June 8th, the correspondent being led through the army on horseback by the provost-marshal guard. On his back and breast were tacked placards inscribed, "Libeller of the Press."

This reporter was Edward Crapsey, correspondent of the Philadelphia Inquirer.*—Ed. 2018*

It was not often, considering the conditions, that correspondents got into trouble in the army. As a rule, they were discreet. Besides this case of Meade, I remember now only one other in which I was actively interested; that was a few months later, after I had returned to the department. Mr. Stanton had been annoyed by a telegram which had been published about Sherman's movements, and he ordered me to send it to the general, so that we might know how much truth there was in it. I wired him as follows:

War Department, November 9, 1864.

Major-General Sherman, Kingston, Ga.:

Following, copied from evening papers, is sent for your information:

Cincinnati, November 9, 1864.

"Yesterday's Indianapolis Journal says : 'Officers from Chattanooga report that Sherman returned to Atlanta early last week with five corps of his army, leaving two corps in Tennessee to watch Hood. He destroyed the railroad from Chattanooga to Atlanta, and is sending the iron into the former place. Atlanta was burned, and Sherman is now marching for Charleston, S.C.'"

Sherman sent back two characteristic dispatches. The first ran:

Kingston, Ga., November 10, 1864.

Hon. C. A. Dana :

Dispatch of 9th read. Can't you send to Indianapolis and catch that fool and have him sent to me to work on the forts? All well.

W. T. Sherman, Major General.

The second:

Kingston, Ga., November 10, 1864.

Hon. C. A. Dana, Assistant Secretary of War:

If indiscreet newspaper men publish information too near the truth, counteract its effect by publishing other paragraphs calculated to mislead the enemy, such as "Sherman's army has been re-enforced, especially in the cavalry, and he will soon move several columns in circuit, so as to catch Hood's army "Sherman's destination is not Charleston, but Selma, where he will meet an army from the Gulf," etc.

W. T. Sherman, Major General.

So I telegraphed to Indianapolis to General A. P. Hovey, who was stationed there:

War Department, November 10, 1864.

Major-General A. P. Hovey, Indianapolis:

In compliance with the request of Major-General Sherman, the Secretary of War directs that you ascertain what persons furnished the information respecting Sherman's alleged movement published in the Indianapolis Journal of the 8th inst. You will arrest them and send them under guard to such point in the Department of the Cumberland as Major-General Thomas may prefer, where they will be employed in hard labor upon the fortifications until General Sherman shall otherwise order.

General Hovey never found the man, however.

By the morning of the 12th of June Grant was ready for his last flank movement of the campaign. Our army at that time, including Sheridan's cavalry, consisted of approximately one hundred and fifteen thousand fighting men. The plan for moving this great body was as follows: The Eighteenth Corps was to move to White House without baggage or artillery, and there embark for City Point. The Fifth Corps was to cross the Chickahominy at Long Bridge, and take a position to secure the passage of the remainder of the army, after which it was to cover the rear. The Second, Sixth, and Ninth Corps were to cross in two columns at Long Bridge and Jones's Bridge. At first it had been hoped, if not opposed by the enemy in force, to strike James River immediately opposite Bermuda Hundred; if resisted, then lower down, where General Butler had been ordered to throw a bridge across and to corduroy the approaches.

The Fifth Corps having prepared the way, the whole army left the lines about Cold Harbor on schedule time, just as soon after nightfall on the 12th as its movements could be concealed from the observation of the enemy. It was in drawing orders for such complicated movements as these, along different roads and by different crossings, that the ability of General Humphreys, the chief of staff, was displayed. Everything went perfectly from the start. That evening at seven o'clock, when I reached Moody's, four miles from Long Bridge, the Fifth Corps (Warren's) was moving rapidly past us. Our cavalry advance, under General Wilson, who had also been transferred to the East, had previously taken Long Bridge and laid a pontoon bridge in readiness for the crossing, so that by nine o'clock that evening the Fifth Corps was south of the Chickahominy, well out toward the approaches from Richmond, and covering them. All day, the 13th, the army was hurrying toward the James. By night the Sixth Corps had reached the river, and the rest of the troops were on the march between there and the Chickahominy, which was our rear.

When I reached the James early the next day, the 14th, large numbers of men were hard at work on the pontoon bridge and its approaches, by which it was intended that the artillery and trains should cross. It was a pretty heavy job to corduroy the marsh, which was fully half a mile wide and quite deep. The bridge itself was unprecedented in military annals, except, perhaps, by that of Xerxes, being nearly seven hundred yards long.

All day on the 14th everything went like a miracle. The pontoon bridge was finished at two o'clock the next morning, and the cavalry of Wilson's leading brigade, followed by the artillery trains, instantly began crossing. By ten o'clock on the 15th Hancock's corps had been ferried over, and he was off toward Petersburg to support Smith, who had taken the Eighteenth Corps around by water from the White House, and had been ordered to attack Petersburg that morning. All the news we had that night at City Point, where headquarters had been set up, was that Smith had assaulted and carried the principal line of the enemy before Petersburg.

The next morning early I was off for the heights southeast of the town. Smith's success appeared to be of the most important kind. He had carried heights which were defended by very formidable works. He thought—and, indeed, we all thought for the moment—that his success gave us perfect command of the city and railroad. I went over the conquered lines with General Grant and the engineer officers, and they all agreed that the works were of the very strongest kind, more difficult even to take than Missionary Ridge at Chattanooga.

General Smith told us that the negro troops fought magnificently, the hardest fighting being done by them. The forts they stormed were, I think, the worst of all. After the affair was over, General Smith went to thank them, and tell them he was proud of their courage and dash. He said they had no superiors as soldiers, and that hereafter he should send them into a difficult place as readily as the best white troops. They captured six out of the sixteen cannons which he took.

It soon appeared, however, that Smith was far from having captured points which commanded Petersburg. His success had but little effect in determining the final result. He had stopped his advance a few minutes and a considerable space too soon, because, as he subsequently alleged, it was too dark and his men were too much fatigued for further operations; and he feared Lee had already re-enforced the town. This turned out not to be so; Lee did not know until the 17th that Grant had crossed the James. And up to that date Lee's position was a mystery to us; we could hardly suppose he had remained at Cold Harbor.

When Grant discovered exactly how much had been gained and lost, he was very much dissatisfied. There was a controversy between Hancock and Smith subsequently about the responsibility for this failure.

On June 16th, the day after Smith's attack, more of the troops arrived before Petersburg. General Meade also arrived on the ground, and the job of capturing Petersburg was now taken up in earnest by the whole Army of the Potomac. It was no longer a mere matter of advancing eighty or one hundred rods, as on the night previous, for meanwhile the enemy had been largely and rapidly re-enforced. Much time and many thousands of valuable lives were to be expended in getting possession of this vital point, which had really been in our grasp on the evening of the 15th. That afternoon there began a series of assaults on the works of the enemy. The fighting lasted all night, the moonlight being very clear. Our loss was heavy.

The next day, the 17th, another attack was made at Petersburg. It was persistent, but Meade found that his men were so worn out with marching, fighting, and digging that they must have rest, and so laid off until noon of the 18th, when, all of the army being up, a general assault was ordered. Nothing important was gained, and General Grant directed that no more assaults should be made. He said that after this he should maneuver to get possession of Petersburg.

I saw nothing of the fighting of June 16th and 17th, being ill in camp, but the members of Grant's staff told me that our operations were unsatisfactory, owing to our previous heavy loss in superior officers. The men fought as well as ever, Colonel Comstock told me, but they were not directed with the same skill and enthusiasm.

While these operations were going on, I made two or three trips to the river to watch the crossing of the troops. It was an animated and inspiring sight, for the great mass of men, animals, and baggage was handled with the greatest intelligence. By the 17th our entire army was south of the James, and the bridge over the river by which the trains had crossed was taken up.

During all this period, from Cold Harbor to Petersburg, we knew nothing of Lee. In making the disposition for this great and successful movement—a far more brilliant evolution than McClellan's "change of base" two years before over almost the same roads—the purpose was, of course, to deceive Lee as to the ultimate direction of the army. The design succeeded far beyond Grant's most sanguine hopes. As soon, on the morning of the 13th, as the Confederate chieftain discovered our withdrawal, he moved his army across the Chickahominy in hot haste, flinging it between his capital and the foe, supposed to be advancing on a new line between the James and the Chickahominy. He held and fortified a line from White Oak swamp to Malvern Hill, and here he remained stock still for four days, wondering what had become of Grant.

Lee had been completely deceived, and could not be made to believe by Beauregard, on the 15th, 16th, and 17th, that Grant's whole army had turned up before Petersburg. His troops, as we know now, did not cross the James, to go to the relief of Beauregard until the 17th. He was caught napping, and, but for mistakes by subordinates in carrying out Grant's plans, Lee's cause would have been lost. In the operations from the night of the 12th, when Grant changed his line and base with an army of one hundred and fifteen thousand men, and all its vast trains of artillery, crossing a wide and deep river on a temporary bridge, until June 18th, when at last Lee awoke to the situation, General Beauregard shines out on the Confederate side far more brilliantly than the general in chief. He unquestionably saved Petersburg, and for the time the Confederacy; but for him Lee had at that time lost the game.

EARLY'S RAID AND THE WASHINGTON PANIC

Although Grant had decided against a further direct attack on the works of Petersburg, he was by no means idle. He sent out expeditions to break up the railroads leading into the town. He began extending his lines around to the south and southwest, so as to make the investment as complete as possible. Batteries were put in place, weak spots in the fortifications were felt for, and regular siege works were begun. Indeed, by July 1st the general opinion seemed to be that the only way we should ever gain Petersburg would be by a systematic siege.

A few days later we had an interesting visit from President Lincoln, who arrived from Washington on June 21st, and at once wanted to visit the lines before Petersburg. General Grant, Admiral Lee, myself, and several others went with him. I remember that, as we passed along the lines, Mr. Lincoln's high hat was brushed off by the branch of a tree. There were a dozen young officers whose duty it was to get it and give it back to the President; but Admiral Lee was off his horse before any of these young chaps, and recovered the hat for the President. Admiral Lee must have been forty-five or fifty years old. It was his agility that impressed me so much.

As we came back we passed through the division of colored troops which had so greatly distinguished itself under Smith on the 15th. They were drawn up in double lines on each side of the road, and they welcomed the President with hearty shouts. It was a memorable thing to behold him whose fortune it was to represent the principle of emancipation passing bareheaded through the enthusiastic ranks of those negroes armed to defend the integrity of the nation.

I went back to Washington with the presidential party, but remained only a few days, as Mr. Lincoln and Mr. Stanton were anxious for my daily reports of the operations around Petersburg. On the return, I arrived at City Point on July 1st. The army occupied about the same positions as when I had left it a week before. Two corps were engaged in siege work, their effort being to get possession of a ridge before them, supposed to command Petersburg; if they succeeded in this, Grant thought that the enemy would have to abandon the south side of the Appomattox, and, of course, the town. On the left our line extended southward and westward across what was known as the Jerusalem road, but at so great a distance from the Confederate fortifications as to have no immediate effect upon them. Farther around to the west, toward the Appomattox above Petersburg, the enemy's works extended, and the idea of enveloping them for the whole distance had been given up. The efforts to break up the railroads leading from Petersburg had been very successful, Grant told me. There were plans for assault suggested, but Grant had not considered any of them seriously.

Before the army had recovered from its long march from Cold Harbor and the failure to capture the town, there was an unusual amount of controversy going on among the officers. Smith was berated generally for failing to complete his attack of June 15th. Butler and "Baldy" Smith were deep in a controversial correspondence; and Meade and Warren were so at loggerheads that Meade notified Warren that he must either ask to be relieved as corps commander or he (Meade) would prefer charges against him. It seemed as if Meade grew more unpopular every day. Finally the difficulties between him and his subordinates became so serious that a change in the commander of the Army of the Potomac seemed probable. Grant had great confidence in Meade, and was much attached to him personally; but the almost universal dislike of Meade which prevailed among officers of every rank who came in contact with him, and the difficulty of doing business with him, felt by everyone except Grant himself, so greatly impaired his capacities for usefulness and rendered success under his command so doubtful that Grant seemed to be coming to the conviction that he must be relieved.

I had long known Meade to be a man of the worst possible temper, especially toward his subordinates. I think he had not a friend in the whole army. No man, no matter what his business or his service, approached him without being insulted in one way or another, and his own staff officers did not dare to speak to him unless first spoken to, for fear of either sneers or curses. The latter, however, I had never heard him indulge in very violently, but he was said to apply them often without occasion and without reason. At the same time, as far as I was able to ascertain, his generals had lost their confidence in him as a commander. His orders for the last series of assaults upon Petersburg, in which we lost ten thousand men without gaining any decisive advantage, were greatly criticized. They were, in effect, that he had found it impracticable to secure the co-operation of corps commanders, and that, therefore, each one was to attack on his own account and do the best he could by himself. The consequence was that each gained some advantage of position, but each exhausted his own strength in so doing; while, for the want of a general purpose and a general commander to direct and concentrate the whole, it all amounted to nothing but heavy loss to ourselves. General Wright remarked confidentially to a friend that all of Meade's attacks had been made without brains and without generalship.

The first week of July the subject came to pretty full discussion at Grant's headquarters on account of an extraordinary correspondence between Meade and Wilson. The Richmond Examiner had charged Wilson's command with stealing not only negroes and horses, but silver plate and clothing on a raid he had just made against the Danville and Southside Railroad, and Meade, taking up the statement of the Examiner for truth, read Wilson a lecture, and called on him for explanations. Wilson denied the charge of robbing women and churches, and said he hoped Meade would not be ready to condemn his command because its operations had excited the ire of the public enemy. Meade replied that Wilson's explanation was satisfactory; but this correspondence started a conversation in which Grant expressed himself quite frankly as to the general trouble with Meade, and his fear that it would become necessary to relieve him. In that event, he said, it would be necessary to put Hancock in command.

In the first days of July we began to get inquiries at City Point from Washington concerning the whereabouts of the Confederate generals Early and Ewell. It was reported in the capital, our dispatches said, that they were moving down the Shenandoah Valley. We seemed to have pretty good evidence that Early was with Lee, defending Petersburg, and so I wired the Secretary on July 3d. The next day we felt less positive. A deserter came in on the morning of the 4th, and said that it was reported in the enemy's camp that Ewell had gone into Maryland with his entire corps. Another twenty-four hours, and Meade told me that he was at last convinced that Early and his troops had gone down the valley. In fact, Early had been gone three weeks. He left Lee's army near Cold Harbor on the morning of the 13th of June, when we were on the march to the James. Hunter's defeat of Jones near Staunton had forced Lee to divide his army in order to stop Hunter's dangerous advance on Lynchburg.

On the 6th General Grant was convinced that Washington was the objective. The raid threatened was sufficiently serious to compel the sending of troops to the defense of the capital, and a body of men immediately embarked. Three days later I started myself to Washington, in order to keep Grant informed of what was going on. When I arrived, I found both Washington and Baltimore in a state of great excitement; both cities were filled with people who had fled from the enemy. The damage to private property done by the invaders was said to be almost beyond calculation. Mills, workshops, and factories of every sort were reported as destroyed, and from twenty-five to fifty miles of the Baltimore and Ohio Railroad torn up.

During my first day in town, July 11th, all sorts of rumors came in. General Lew Wallace, then in command at Baltimore, sent word that a large force of the enemy had been seen that morning near that city. The Confederate generals were said to have dined together at Rockville a day or two before. The houses of Governor Bradford, Francis P. Blair, senior, and his son, Montgomery, the Postmaster General, were reported burned. We could see from Washington clouds of dust in several quarters around the city, which we believed to be raised by bodies of hostile cavalry. There was some sharp skirmishing that day, too, on the Tennallytown road, as well as later in front of Fort Stevens, and at night the telegraph operators at the latter place reported a considerable number of camp fires visible in front of them.

I found that the Washington authorities had utilized every man in town for defense. Some fifteen hundred employees of the quartermaster's department had been armed and sent out; the veteran reserves about Washington and Alexandria had likewise been sent to the front. General Augur, commanding the defenses of Washington, had also drawn from the fortifications on the south side of the town all the men that in his judgment could possibly be spared. To this improvised force were added that day some six boatloads of troops which General Grant had sent from the Army of the Potomac. These troops went at once to Fort Stevens.

With the troops coming from Grant, there was force enough to save the capital; but I soon saw that nothing could possibly be done toward pursuing or cutting off the enemy for want of a commander. General Hunter and his forces had not yet returned from their swing around the circle. General Augur commanded the defenses of Washington, with A. McD. McCook and a lot of brigadier generals under him, but he was not allowed to go outside. Wright commanded only his own corps. General Gilmore had been assigned to the temporary command of those troops of the Nineteenth Corps just arrived from New Orleans, and all other troops in the Middle Department, leaving Wallace to command Baltimore alone. But there was no head to the whole. General Halleck would not give orders, except as he received them from Grant; the President would give none; and, until Grant directed positively and explicitly what was to be done, everything was practically at a standstill. Things, I saw, would go on in the deplorable and fatal way in which they had been going for a week. Of course, this want of a head was causing a great deal of sharp comment on all sides. Postmaster-General Blair was particularly incensed, and, indeed, with real cause, for he had lost his house at Silver Springs. Some of his remarks reached General Halleck, who immediately wrote to Mr. Stanton the following letter:

Headquarters of the Army,

Washington, July 13, 1864.

Hon. E. M. Stanton, Secretary of War.

Sir: I deem it my duty to bring to your notice the following facts: I am informed by an officer of rank and standing in the military service that the Hon. M. Blair, Postmaster General, in speaking of the burning of his house in Maryland this morning, said, in effect, that the officers in command about Washington are poltroons; that there were not more than five hundred rebels on the Silver Springs road, and we had one million of men in arms; that it was a disgrace; that General Wallace was in comparison with them far better, as he would at least fight. As there have been for the last few days a large number of officers on duty in and about Washington who have devoted their time and energies, night and day, and have periled their lives in the support of the Government, it is due to them, as well as to the War Department, that it should be known whether such wholesale denouncement and accusation by a member of the Cabinet receives the sanction and approbation of the President of the United States. If so, the names of the officers accused should be stricken from the rolls of the army; if not, it is due to the honor of the accused that the slanderer should be dismissed from the Cabinet.

Very respectfully, your obedient servant,

H. W. Halleck,

Major General and Chief of Staff.

The very day on which Halleck wrote this letter we had evidence that the enemy had taken fright at the arrival in Washington of the troops sent by Grant, and were moving off toward Edwards Ferry. It was pretty certain that they were carrying off a large amount of cattle and other plunder with them. By the end of another day there seemed no doubt that Early had got the main body of his command across the river with his captures. What they were, it was impossible to say precisely. One herd of cattle was reported as containing two thousand head, and the number of horses and mules taken from Maryland was reported as about five thousand. This, however, was probably somewhat exaggerated.

The veterans, of course, at once moved out to attempt to overtake the enemy. The irregulars were withdrawn from the fortifications, General Meigs marching his division of quartermaster's clerks and employees back to their desks; and Admiral Goldsborough, who had marshalled the marines and sailors, returned to smoke his pipe on his own doorstep.

Montgomery Cunningham Meigs (1816 – 1892) was one of the great unsung heroes of the war. As Quartermaster General of the Army, he disbursed vast sums of money and managed supplies and logistics on a scale previously unknown. He was lauded for his ability to prevent loss and promote efficiency.—Ed. 2018

The pursuit of Early proved, on the whole, an egregious blunder, relieved only by a small success at Winchester in which four guns and some prisoners were captured. Wright accomplished nothing, and drew back as soon as he got where he might have done something worthwhile. As it was, Early escaped with the whole of his plunder.

One of the best letters Grant sent me during the war was at the time of this Early raid on Washington. When the alarms of invasion first came, Grant ordered Major-General David Hunter, then stationed at Parkersburg, W. Va., to take the direction of operations against the enemy's forces in the valley. Hunter did not come up to Mr. Stanton's expectations in this crisis, and when I reached Washington the Secretary told me to telegraph Grant that, in his opinion, Hunter ought to be removed. Three days later I repeated in my dispatch to Grant certain rumors about Hunter that had reached the War Department. The substance of them was that Hunter had been engaged in an active campaign against the newspapers in West Virginia, and that he had horsewhipped a soldier with his own hand. I received an immediate reply:

City Point, Va., July 15, 1864—8 p. m.

C. A. Dana, Assistant Secretary of War:

I am sorry to see such a disposition to condemn so brave an old soldier as General Hunter is known to be without a hearing. He is known to have advanced into the enemy's country toward their main army, inflicting a much greater damage upon them than they have inflicted upon us with double his force, and moving directly away from our main army. Hunter acted, too, in a country where we had no friends, while the enemy have only operated in territory where, to say the least, many of the inhabitants are their friends. If General Hunter has made war upon the newspapers in West Virginia, probably he has done right. In horsewhipping a soldier he has laid himself subject to trial, but nine chances out of ten he only acted on the spur of the moment, under great provocation. I fail to see yet that General Hunter has not acted with great promptness and great success. Even the enemy give him great credit for courage, and congratulate themselves that he will give them a chance of getting even with him.

U. S. Grant, Lieutenant General.

THE SECRET SERVICE OF THE WAR.

After Early's invaders had retired and quiet was restored, I went to Mr. Stanton for new orders. As there was no probability of an immediate change in the situation before Petersburg, the Secretary did not think it necessary for me to go back to Grant, but preferred that I remain in the department, helping with the routine work.

Much of my time at this period was spent in investigating charges against defaulting contractors and dishonest agents, and in ordering arrests of persons suspected of disloyalty to the Government. I assisted, too, in supervising the spies who were going back and forth between the lines. Among these I remember one, a sort of peddler—whose name I will call Morse—who traveled between Washington and Richmond. When he went down it was in the character of a man who had entirely hoodwinked the Washington authorities, and who, in spite of them, or by some corruption or other, always brought with him into the Confederate lines something that the people wanted— dresses for the ladies or some little luxury that they couldn't get otherwise. The things that he took with him were always supervised by our agents before he went away. When he came back he brought us in exchange a lot of valuable information. He was doubtless a spy on both sides; but as we got a great deal of information, which could be had in no other way, about the strength of the Confederate armies, and the preparations and the movements of the enemy, we allowed the thing to go on. The man really did good service for us that summer, and, as we were frequently able to verify by other means the important information he brought, we had a great deal of confidence in him.

Early in October, 1864, he came back from Richmond, and, as usual, went to Baltimore to get his outfit for the return trip. When he presented himself again in Washington, the chief detective of the War Department, Colonel [Lafayette] Baker, examined his goods carefully, but this time he found that Morse had many things that we could not allow him to take. Among his stuff were uniforms and other military goods, and all this, of course, was altogether too contraband to be passed. We had all his bills, telling where he had bought these things in Baltimore. They amounted to perhaps twenty-five thousand dollars, or more. So we confiscated the contraband goods, and put Morse in prison.

But the merchants in Baltimore were partners in his guilt, and Secretary Stanton declared he would arrest every one of them and put them in prison until the affair could be straightened up. He turned the matter over to me then, as he was going to Fort Monroe for a few days. I immediately sent Assistant-Adjutant-General Lawrence to Baltimore with orders to see that all persons implicated were arrested. Lawrence telegraphed me, on October 16th, that the case would involve the arrest of two hundred citizens. I reported to the Secretary, but he was determined to go ahead. The next morning ninety-seven of the leading citizens of Baltimore were arrested, brought to Washington, and confined in Old Capitol Prison, principally in solitary cells. There was great satisfaction among the Union people of the town, but great indignation among Southern sympathizers. Presently a deputation from Baltimore came over to see President Lincoln. It was an outrage, they said; the gentlemen arrested were most respectable merchants and faultless citizens, and they demanded that they all be set instantly at liberty and damages paid them. Mr. Lincoln sent the deputation over to the War Department, and Mr. Stanton, who had returned by this time, sent for me. "All Baltimore is coming here" he said. "Sit down and hear the discussion."

They came in, the bank presidents and boss merchants of Baltimore—there must have been at least fifty million dollars represented in the deputation—and sat down around the fire in the Secretary's office. Presently they began to make their speeches, detailing the circumstances and the wickedness of this outrage. There was no ground for it, they said, no justification. After half a dozen of them had spoken, Mr. Stanton asked one after another if he had anything more to say, and they all said no. Then Stanton began, and delivered one of the most eloquent speeches that I ever heard. He described the beginning of the war, for which, he said, there was no justification; being beaten in an election was no reason for destroying the Government. Then he went on to the fact that half a million of our young men had been laid in untimely graves by this conspiracy of the slave interest. He outlined the whole conspiracy in the most solemn and impressive terms, and then he depicted the offense that this man Morse, aided by these several merchants, had committed. "Gentlemen," he said, "if you would like to examine the bills of what he was taking to the enemy, here they are."

When Stanton had finished, these gentlemen, without answering a word, got up and one by one went away. That was the only speech I ever listened to that cleared out the entire audience.

Early in the winter of 1863-64 a curious thing happened in the secret service of the War Department. Sometime in the February or March before, a slender and prepossessing young fellow, between twenty-two and twenty-six apparently, had applied at the War Department for employment as a spy within the Confederate lines.

The main body of the Army of Northern Virginia was then lying at Gordonsville, and the headquarters of the Army of the Potomac were at Culpeper Courthouse. General Grant had not yet come from the West to take command of the momentous campaign which afterward opened with his movement into the Wilderness on the 5th of May.

The young man who sought this terrible service was well dressed and intelligent, and professed to be animated by motives purely patriotic. He was a clerk in one of the departments. All that he asked was that he should have a horse and an order which would carry him safely through the Federal lines, and, in return, he undertook to bring information from General Lee's army and from the Government of the Confederacy in Richmond. He understood perfectly the perilous nature of the enterprise he proposed.

Finding that the applicant bore a good character in the office where he was employed, it was determined to accept his proposal. He was furnished with a horse, an order that would pass him through the Union lines, and also, I believe, with a moderate sum of money, and then he departed. Two or three weeks later he reported at the War Department. He had been in Gordonsville and Richmond, had obtained the confidence of the Confederate authorities, and was the bearer of a letter from Mr. Jefferson Davis to [Mr. Clement C. Clay](), the agent of the Confederate Government in Canada, then known to be stationed at St. Catherine's, not far from Niagara Falls. Mr. Clay had as his official associate Jacob Thompson, of Mississippi, who had been Secretary of the Interior in the Cabinet of President Buchanan, and, like Mr. Clay, had been serving the Confederate Government ever since its organization.

The letter from Mr. Davis the young man exhibited, but only the outside of the envelope was examined.

The address was in the handwriting of the Confederate chief, and the statement of our young adventurer that it was merely a letter of recommendation advising Messrs. Clay and Thompson that they might repose confidence in the bearer, since he was ardently devoted to the Confederate cause and anxious to serve the great purpose that it had in view, appeared entirely probable; so the young man was allowed to proceed to Niagara Falls and Canada. He made some general report upon the condition of the rebel army at Gordonsville, but it was of no particular value, except that in its more interesting features it agreed with our information from other sources.

Our spy was not long in returning from St. Catherine's with a dispatch which was also allowed to pass unopened, upon his assurance that it contained nothing of importance. In this way he went back and forward from Richmond to St. Catherine's once or twice. We supplied him with money to a limited extent, and also with one or two more horses. He said that he got some money from the Confederates, but had not thought it prudent to accept from them anything more than very small sums, since his professed zeal for the Confederate cause forbade his receiving anything for his traveling expenses beyond what was absolutely necessary.

During the summer of 1864 the activity of Grant's campaign, and the fighting which prevailed all along the line, somewhat impeded our young man's expeditions, but did not stop them. All his subsequent dispatches, however, whether coming from Richmond or from Canada, were regularly brought to the War Department, and were opened, and in every case a copy of them was kept. As it was necessary to break the seals and destroy the envelopes in opening them, there was some difficulty in sending them forward in what should appear to be the original wrappers. Coming from Canada, the paper employed was English, and there was a good deal of trouble in procuring paper of the same appearance. I remember also that one important dispatch, which was sealed with Mr. Clay's seal, had to be delayed somewhat while we had an imitation seal engraved. But these delays were easily accounted for at Richmond by the pretense that they had been caused by accidents upon the road and by the necessity of avoiding the Federal pickets. At any rate, the confidence of the Confederates in our agent and in theirs never seemed to be shaken by any of these occurrences.

Finally our dispatch bearer reported one day at the War Department with a document which, he said, was of extraordinary consequence. It was found to contain an account of a scheme for setting fire to New York and Chicago by means of clock-work machines that were to be placed in several of the large hotels and places of amusement—particularly in Barnum's Museum in New York—and to be set off simultaneously, so that the fire department in each place would be unable to attend to the great number of calls that would be made upon it on account of these Confederate conflagrations in so many different quarters, and thus these cities might be greatly damaged, or even destroyed.

This dispatch was duly sealed up again and was taken to Richmond, and a confidential officer was at once sent to New

York to warn General Dix, who was in command there, of the Confederate project. The general was very unwilling to believe that any such design could be seriously entertained, and Mr. John A. Kennedy, then superintendent of police, was equally incredulous. But the Secretary of War was peremptory in his orders, and when the day of the incendiary attempt arrived both the military and the police made every preparation to prevent the threatened catastrophe. The officer who went from Washington was lodged in the St. Nicholas Hotel, one of the large establishments that were to be set on fire, and while he was washing his hands in the evening, preparatory to going to dinner, a fire began burning in the room next to his. It was promptly put out, and was found to be caused by a clock-work apparatus which had been left in that room by a lodger who had departed some hours before. Other fires likewise occurred. In every instance these fires were extinguished without much damage and without exciting any considerable public attention, thanks to the precautions that had been taken in consequence of the warning derived from Mr. Clay's dispatch to Mr. Benjamin in Richmond. The plan of setting fire to Chicago proved even more abortive; I do not remember that any report of actual burning was received from there.

Later in the fall, after the military operations had substantially terminated for the season, a dispatch was brought from Canada, signed by Mr. Clay, and addressed to Mr. Benjamin, as Secretary of State in the Confederate Government, conveying the information that a new and really formidable military expedition against northern Vermont—particularly against Burlington, if I am not mistaken—had been organized and fitted out in Canada, and would make its attack as soon as practicable. This was after the well-known attempt upon St. Albans and Lake Champlain, on October 19, 1864, and promised to be much more injurious. The dispatch reached Washington one Sunday morning, and was brought to the War Department as usual, but its importance in the eyes of the Confederate agents had led to its being prepared for transportation with uncommon care. It was placed between two thicknesses of the pair of re-enforced cavalry trousers which the messenger wore, and sewed up so that when he was mounted it was held between his thigh and the saddle.

Having been carefully ripped out and opened, it was immediately carried to Mr. Stanton, who was confined to his house by a cold. He read it. "This is serious," he said. "Go over to the White House and ask the President to come here." Mr. Lincoln was found dressing to go to church, and he was soon driven to Mr. Stanton's house. After discussing the subject in every aspect, and considering thoroughly the probability that to keep the dispatch would put an end to communications by this channel, they determined that it must be kept. The conclusive reason for this step was that it established beyond question the fact that the Confederates, while sheltering themselves behind the British Government in Canada, had organized and fitted out a military expedition against the United States. But while the dispatch afforded evidence that could not be gainsaid, the mere possession of it was not sufficient. It must be found in the possession of the Confederate dispatch bearer, and the circumstances attending its capture must be established in such a manner that the British Foreign Office would not be able to dispute the genuineness of the document. "We must have this paper for Seward," said Mr. Lincoln. "As for the young man, get him out of the scrape if you can." Accordingly, the paper was taken back to the War Department and sewed up again in the trousers whence it had been taken three hours before. The bearer was instructed to start at dusk on the road which he usually took in passing through the lines, to be at a certain tavern outside of Alexandria at nine o'clock in the evening, and to stop there to water his horse. Then information was sent through Major-General Augur, commandant of Washington and the surrounding region, to Colonel Henry H. Wells, then provost marshal general of the defenses south of the Potomac, stationed at Alexandria, directing him to be at this tavern at nine o'clock in the evening, and to arrest a Confederate dispatch bearer, concerning whom authentic information had been received at the War Department, and whose description was furnished for his (Wells's) guidance. He was to do the messenger no injury, but to make sure of his person and of all papers that he might have upon him, and to bring him under a sufficient guard directly to the War Department. And General Augur was directed to be present there, in order to assist in the examination of the prisoner, and to verify any dispatches that might be found.

Just before midnight a carriage drove up to the door of the War Department with a soldier on the box and two soldiers on the front seat within, while the back seat was occupied by Colonel Wells and the prisoner. Of course, no one but the two or three who had been in the secret was aware that this gentleman had walked quietly out of the War Department only a few hours previously, and that the paper which was the cause of the entire ceremony had been sewed up in his clothes just before his departure. Colonel Wells reported that, while the prisoner had offered no resistance, he was very violent and outrageous in his language, and that he boasted fiercely of his devotion to the Confederacy and his detestation of the Union. During the examination which now followed he said nothing except to answer a few questions, but his bearing—patient, scornful, undaunted—was that of an incomparable actor. If Mr. Clay and Mr. Benjamin had been present, they would have been more than ever certain that he was one of their noblest young men. His hat, boots, and other articles of his clothing were taken off one by one. The hat and boots were first searched, and finally the dispatch was found in his trousers and taken out. Its nature and the method of its capture were stated in a memorandum which was drawn up on the spot and signed by General Augur and Colonel Wells and one or two other officers who were there for the purpose, and then the dispatch bearer himself was sent off to the Old Capitol Prison.

The dispatch, with the documents of verification, was handed over to Mr. Seward for use in London, and a day or two afterward the warden of the Old Capitol Prison was directed to give the dispatch bearer an opportunity of escaping, with a proper show of attempted prevention. One afternoon the spy walked into my office. "Ah!" said I, "you have run away."

"Yes, sir," he answered.

"Did they shoot at you?"

"They did, and didn't hit me; but I didn't think that would answer the purpose. So I shot myself through the arm."

He showed me the wound. It was through the fleshy part of the forearm, and due care had been taken not to break any bones. A more deliberate and less dangerous wound could not be, and yet it did not look trivial.

He was ordered to get away to Canada as promptly as possible, so that he might explain the loss of his dispatch before it should become known there by any other means. An advertisement offering two thousand dollars for his recapture was at once inserted in the New York *Herald*, the Pittsburgh *Journal*, and the Chicago *Tribune*. No one ever appeared to claim the reward, but in about a week the escaped prisoner returned from Canada with new dispatches that had been entrusted to him. They contained nothing of importance, however. The wound in his arm had borne testimony in his favor, and the fact that he had hurried through to St. Catherine's without having it dressed was thought to afford conclusive evidence of his fidelity to the Confederate cause.

The war was ended soon after this adventure, and, as his services had been of very great value, a new place, with the assurance of lasting employment, was found for the young man in one of the bureaus of the War Department. He did not remain there very long, however, and I don't know what became of him. He was one of the cleverest creatures I ever saw. His style of patriotic lying was sublime; it amounted to genius.

A VISIT TO SHERIDAN IN THE VALLEY

It was just after the arrest of the Baltimore merchants, in October, 1864, that I visited Sheridan at his headquarters in the Shenandoah Valley. He had finished the work of clearing out the valley by the battle of Cedar Creek on October 19th, and the Government wanted to recognize the victory by promoting him to the rank of major general in the regular army. There were numerous volunteer officers who were also officers in the regular army, and it was regarded as a considerable distinction. The appointment was made, and then, as an additional compliment to General Sheridan, instead of sending him the commission by an ordinary officer from the department, Mr. Stanton decided that I would better deliver it. I started on October 22d, going by special train to Harper's Ferry, whither I telegraphed for an escort to be ready for me. I was delayed so that I did not get started from Harper's Ferry until about five o'clock on the morning of October 23d. It was a distance of about fifty miles to Sheridan, and by riding all day I got there about eleven o'clock at night. Sheridan had gone to bed, but in time of war one never delays in carrying out orders, whatever their nature. The general was awakened, and soon was out of his tent; and there, by the flare of an army torch and in the presence of a few sleepy aides-de-camp and of my own tired escort, I presented to Sheridan his commission as major general in the regular army.

Sheridan did not say much in reply to my little speech, nor could he have been expected to under the circumstances, though he showed lively satisfaction in the Government's appreciation of his services, and spoke most heartily, I remember, of the manner in which the administration had always supported him.

The morning after this little ceremony, when we had finished our breakfast, the general asked me if I would not like to ride through the army with him. It was exactly what I did want to do, and we were soon on horseback and off, accompanied by four of his officers. We rode through the entire army that morning, dismounting now and then to give me an opportunity to pay my respects to several officers whom I knew. I was struck, in riding through the lines, by the universal demonstration of personal affection for Sheridan. Everybody seemed personally to be attached to him. He was like the most popular man after an election—the whole force everywhere honored him. Finally I said to the general: "I wish you would explain one thing to me. Here I find all these people of every rank—generals, sergeants, corporals, and private soldiers; in fact, everybody—manifesting a personal affection for you that I have never seen in any other army, not even in the Army of the Tennessee for Grant. I have never seen anything like it. Tell me what is the reason?"

"Mr. Dana," said he, "I long ago made up my mind that it was not a good plan to fight battles with paper orders—that is, for the commander to stand on a hill in the rear and send his aides-de-camp with written orders to the different commanders. My practice has always been to fight in the front rank."

"Well," said I, "General, that is dangerous; in the front rank a man is much more liable to be killed than he is in the rear."

"Well," said he, "I know that there is a certain risk in it; but, in my judgment, the advantage is much greater than the risk, and I have come to the conclusion that that is the right thing to do. That is the reason the men like me. They know that when the hard pinch comes I am exposed just as much as any of them."

"But are you never afraid?" I asked.

"If I was I should not be ashamed of it," he said. "If I should follow my natural impulse, I should run away always at the beginning of the danger; the men who say they are never afraid in a battle do not tell the truth."

I talked a great deal with Sheridan and his officers while at Cedar Creek on the condition of the valley, and as to what should be done to hold it. The active campaign seemed to be over in this region for that year. The enemy were so decidedly beaten and scattered, and driven so far to the south, that they could scarcely be expected to collect their forces for another attempt during the season. Besides, the devastation of the valley, extending as it did for a distance of about one hundred miles, rendered it almost impossible that either the Confederates or our own forces should make a new campaign in that territory. It looked to me as if, when Sheridan had completed the same process down the valley to the vicinity of the Potomac, and when the stores of forage which were yet to be found were all destroyed or removed, the difficulty of any new offensive operations on either side would be greatly increased.

The key to the Shenandoah Valley was, in Sheridan's judgment, the line of the Opequan Creek, which was rather a deep canon that an ordinary watercourse. Sheridan's idea I understood to be to fall back to the proper defensive point upon that creek, and there to construct fortifications which would effectually cover the approach to the Potomac.

I left Sheridan at Cedar Creek, and went back to Washington by way of Manassas Gap.

All through the fall of 1864 and the following winter I remained in Washington, very much occupied with the regular routine business of the department and various matters of incidental interest. Some of these incidents I shall group together here, without strict regard to sequence.

An important part of the work of the department was in relation to the railroads and to railroad transportation. Sometimes it was a whole army corps to be moved. At another time the demand would be equally sudden and urgent, if less vital to the Union cause. I remember particularly the great turkey movement in November of that year. The presidential election was hardly over before the people of the North began to prepare Thanksgiving boxes for the army. George Bliss, Jr., of New York, telegraphed me, on November 16th, that they had twenty thousand turkeys ready in that city to send to the front; and the next day, fearing, I suppose, that that wasn't enough, he wired: "It would be a very great convenience in our turkey business if I could know definitely the approximate number of men in each of armies of Potomac, James, and Shenandoah, respectively."

From Philadelphia I received a message asking for transportation to Sheridan's army for "boxes containing four thousand turkeys, and Heaven knows what else, as a Thanksgiving dinner for the brave fellows." And so it was from all over the country. The North not only poured out food and clothing generously for our own men, but, when Savannah was entered by Sherman, great quantities of provisions were sent there for gratuitous distribution, and when Charleston fell every effort was made to relieve destitution.

A couple of months later, in January, 1865, a piece of work not so different from the "turkey business," but on a rather larger scale, fell to me. This was the transfer of the Twenty-third Army Corps, commanded by Major-General John M. Schofield, from its position on the Tennessee River to Chesapeake Bay. There being no prospect of a winter campaign under Thomas, Grant had ordered the corps transferred as quickly as possible, and Mr. Stanton turned over the direction to me. On January 10th I telegraphed to Grant at City Point the plan to be followed. This, briefly, was to send Colonel Lewis B. Parsons, chief of railroad and river transportation, to the West to take charge of the corps. I proposed to move the whole body by boats to Parkersburg if navigation allowed, and thence by the Baltimore and Ohio Railroad to Annapolis, for I remembered well with what promptness and success Hooker's forces, the Eleventh and Twelfth Corps, were moved into Tennessee in 1863 by that road. A capital advantage of that line was that it avoided all large towns—and the temptations of large towns were bad for the soldiers in transit. If the Ohio River should be frozen,

I proposed to move the corps by rail from Cairo, Evansville, and Jeffersonville to Parkersburg or Bellaire, according to circumstances.

Commanders in the vicinity of the corps were advised of the change, and ordered to prepare steamboats and transports. Loyal officers of railroads were requested to meet Colonel Parsons at given points to arrange for the concentration of rolling stock in case the river could not be used. Liquor shops were ordered closed along the route, and arrangements were made for the comfort of the troops by supplying to them, , as often as once in every hundred miles of travel, an abundance of hot coffee in addition to their rations.

Colonel Parsons proceeded at once to Louisville, where he arrived on the 13th. By the morning of the 18th he had started the first division from the mouth of the Tennessee up the Ohio, and had transportation ready for the rest of the corps. He then hurried to Cincinnati, where, as the river was too full of ice to permit a further transfer by water, he loaded about three thousand men on the cars waiting there and started them eastward. The rest of the corps rapidly followed. In spite of fogs and ice on the river, and broken rails and machinery on the railroads, the entire army corps was encamped on the banks of the Potomac on February 2d.

The distance over which the corps was transported was nearly fourteen hundred miles, about equally divided between land and water. The average time of transportation, from the embarkment on the Tennessee to the arrival on the banks of the Potomac, did not exceed eleven days; and what was still more important was the fact that during the whole movement not a single accident happened causing loss of life, limb, or property, except in a single instance where a soldier improperly jumped from the car, under apprehension of danger, and thus lost his life. Had he remained quiet, he would have been as safe as were his comrades of the same car.

Much of the success of the movement was due to the hearty co-operation of J. W. Garrett, president of the Baltimore and Ohio Railroad. Colonel Parsons did not say too much when he wrote, in his report of the transfer of Schofield's troops:

The circumstances, I think, render it not invidious that I should especially refer to the management of the Baltimore and Ohio Railroad, where indomitable will, energy, and superior ability have been so often and so conspicuously manifested, and where such invaluable service has been rendered to the Government; a road nearly four hundred miles in length, so often broken and apparently destroyed, so constantly subjected to rebel incursions, that, had it been under ordinary management, it would long since have ceased operation; yet, notwithstanding all the difficulties of the severe winter season, the great disorganization of employees necessarily incident to a road thus situated, its most extraordinary curves, grades, bridges, tunnels, and the mountain heights it scales, it has moved this large force in the shortest possible time, with almost the exactness and regularity of ordinary passenger trains, and with a freedom from accident that, I think, has seldom, if ever, been paralleled.

At the end of the war, when the department's energies were devoted to getting itself as quickly and as thoroughly as possible upon a peace footing, it fell to me to examine the condition of the numerous railroads which the Government had seized and used in the time of active military operations, and to recommend what was to be done with them. This readjustment was not the least difficult of the complicated questions of disarmament. The Government had spent millions of dollars on improvements to some of these military railroads while operating them. My report was not finished till late in May, 1865, and as it contains much out-of-the-way information on the subject, and has never been published, I introduce it here in full:

Washington City, May 29, 1865.

Hon. Edwin M. Stanton, Secretary of War.

Sir: I have the honor to report that I have examined the subject of the disposition to be made of the railroads in the States lately in rebellion, referred to me in connection with the report of the quartermaster general, and the rules which he has recommended to be established. The second rule proposed by the quartermaster general provides that no charge shall be made against a railroad for expense of materials or expense of operation while it has been in the hands of the military authorities of the United States. In other words, he proposes to restore every railroad to its claimants without any special consideration from them for any improvements which the United States may have made upon it.

It is true in his fourth rule he includes past expenditures of defense and repair as an equivalent for the use of the road while it has been in the public service, but in many cases this does not appear to me to be sufficient. Our expenditures upon some of these roads have been very heavy. For instance, we have added to the value of the road from Nashville to Chattanooga at least a million and a half dollars. When that road was recaptured from the public enemy it was in a very bad state of repair. Its embankments were in many places partially washed away, its iron was what is known as the U rail, and was laid in the defective old-fashioned manner, upon longitudinal sleepers, without cross ties. These sleepers were also in a state of partial decay, so that trains could not be run with speed or safety. All these defects have now been remedied. The roadbed has been placed in first-rate condition. The iron is now a heavy T rail, laid in new iron the entire length of the line. Extensive repair shops have also been erected, well furnished with the necessary tools and machinery. I do not conceive that it would be just or advisable to restore this road, with its improved tracks and these costly shops, without any equivalent for the great value of these improvements other than the use we have made of it since its recapture. The fact that we have replaced the heavy and expensive bridges over Elk, Duck, and Tennessee Rivers, and over Running Water Creek, should also not be forgotten in deciding this question.

The above general remarks are also applicable to that portion of the Orange and Alexandria Railroad between the Potomac and the Rapidan. Very extensive repair shops have been erected at Alexandria, and furnished with costly machinery for the use of the road, and I understand that the iron and the roadbed are now much better than when the Government began to use it.

The same is still more the case with the road between City Point and Petersburg. When that road was recaptured from the public enemy not only was the roadbed a good deal washed away and damaged, but neither rails nor sound ties were left upon it. Now it is in the best possible condition. Can anyone contend that it ought to be restored to its claimants without charge for the new ties and iron?

The case of the railroad from Harper's Ferry to Winchester is no less striking. It was a very poor road before the war, and was early demolished by the rebels. Not a pound of iron, not a sound tie, was to be found upon the line when we began its reconstruction in

December last. We have spent about five hundred thousand dollars in bringing it to its present condition, and I have no doubt our improvements could be sold for that sum to the Baltimore and Ohio Company should they obtain the title to the roadbed from the proper authorities of Virginia. Why, then, should we give them up for nothing?

On the Morehead City and Goldsboro' Railroad we have rebuilt twenty-seven miles of the track, and furnished it with new iron and laid new ties on many miles more since February last. These views also hold good, unless I am misinformed, with regard to the railroad leading into New Orleans, the Memphis and Little Rock Railroad, the Memphis and Charleston Railroad, and the Mobile and Ohio Railroad. They have all been improved at great expense while in our hands.

In the third rule proposed by the quartermaster general it is provided that all materials for permanent way used in the repair and construction of any road, and all damaged material of this class which may be left along its route, having been thrown there during operation of destruction and repair, shall be considered as part of the road, and given up with it also without compensation. If this means to give up any new iron that we have on the line of any road, it seems to me to concede to the parties to whom the roads are to be surrendered more than they have a right to claim. For instance, there is now lying at Alexandria, on the line of the Orange and Alexandria road, iron sufficient to lay thirty miles of track. It seems manifest to me that this iron should not be surrendered to the road without being paid for. In my judgment it is also advisable to establish the principle that the Government will not pay for the damages done any road in the prosecution of hostilities, any more than it will pay for similar damages done by the enemy. With these exceptions, the principles proposed by the quartermaster general appear to be correct.

In accordance with these observations, I would recommend that the following rules be determined upon to govern the settlement of these matters:

1. The United States will, as soon as it can dispense with military occupation and control of any road of which the Quartermaster's Department is in charge, turn it over to the parties asking to receive it who may appear to have the best claim, and be able to operate it

in such a manner as to secure the speedy movement of all military stores and troops, the quartermaster general, upon the advice of the commander of the department, to determine when this can be done, subject to the approval of the Secretary of War.

2. Where any State has a loyal board of works, or other executive officers charged with the supervision of railroads, such road shall be turned over to such board of officers rather than to any corporations or private parties.

3. When any railroad shall be so turned over, a board of appraisers shall be appointed, who shall estimate and determine the value of any improvements which may have been made by the United States, either in the road itself or in its repair shop and permanent machinery, and the amount of such improvements shall be a lien upon the road.

4. The parties to whom the road is turned over shall have the option of purchasing at their value any tools, iron, or any other materials for permanent way which have been provided by the United States for the improvement of the road and have not been used.

5. All other movable property, including rolling stock of all kinds, the property of the United States, to be sold at auction, after full public notice, to the highest bidder.

6. All rolling stock and materials of railroads captured by the forces of the United States, and not consumed, destroyed, or permanently fixed elsewhere—as, for instance, when captured iron has been laid upon other roads—shall be placed at the disposal of the roads which originally owned them, and shall be given up to these roads as soon as it can be spared and they appear by proper agents authorized to receive it.

7. No payment or credit shall be given to any railroad recaptured from the enemy for its occupation or use by the United States to take possession of it, but its capture and restoration shall be considered a sufficient consideration for all such use; nor shall any indemnity be paid for injuries done to the property of any road by the forces of the United States during the continuance of the war.

8. Roads which have not been operated by the United States Quartermaster's Department not to be interfered with unless under military necessity; such roads to be left in the possession of such

persons as may now have possession, subject only to the removal of every agent, director, president, superintendent, or operative who has not taken the oath of allegiance to the United States. g. When superintendents in actual possession decline to take the oath, some competent person shall be appointed as receiver of the road, who will administer its affairs and account for its receipts to the board of directors, who may be formally recognized as the legal and formal board of managers, the receiver to be appointed by the Treasury Department, as in the case of abandoned property.

I am, sir, very respectfully, your obedient servant,

C. A. Dana,

Assistant Secretary of War.

These recommendations were carried out partly in the transfer, which was practically complete by the end of 1865. The department decided upon a somewhat more liberal policy than I had thought justifiable. The roads and bridges were transferred practically in the same condition as they were in at the time of transfer. It was believed that this generosity would react favorably upon the revenue and credit of the nation, and there is no doubt that it did have a good influence.

During the presidential campaign of 1864, which resulted in Lincoln's re-election and in the further prosecution of the war upon the lines of Lincoln's policy, we were busy in the department arranging for soldiers to go home to vote, and also for the taking of ballots in the army. There was a constant succession of telegrams from all parts of the country requesting that leave of absence be extended to this or that officer, in order that his district at home might have the benefit of his vote and political influence. Furloughs were asked for private soldiers whose presence in close districts was deemed of especial importance, and there was a widespread demand that men on detached service and convalescents in hospitals be sent home.

All the power and influence of the War Department, then something enormous from the vast expenditure and extensive relations of the war, was employed to secure the re-election of Mr. Lincoln. The political struggle was most intense, and the interest taken in it, both in the White House and in the War Department, was almost painful. After the arduous toil of the canvass, there was naturally a great suspense of feeling until the result of the voting should be ascertained. On November 8th, election day, I went over to the War Department about half past eight o'clock in the evening, and found the President and Mr. Stanton together in the Secretary's office. General Eckert, who then had charge of the telegraph department of the War Office, was coming in constantly with telegrams containing election returns. Mr. Stanton would read them, and the President would look at them and comment upon them. Presently there came a lull in the returns, and Mr. Lincoln called me to a place by his side.

"Dana," said he, "have you ever read any of the writings of [humorist] Petroleum V. Nasby?"

"No, sir," I said; "I have only looked at some of them, and they seemed to be quite funny."

"Well," said he, "let me read you a specimen"; and, pulling out a thin yellow-covered pamphlet from his breast pocket, he began to read aloud. Mr. Stanton viewed these proceedings with great impatience, as I could see, but Mr. Lincoln paid no attention to that. He would read a page or a story, pause to consider a new election telegram, and then open the book again and go ahead with a new passage. Finally, Mr. Chase came in, and presently somebody else, and then the reading was interrupted.

Mr. Stanton went to the door and beckoned me into the next room. I shall never forget the fire of his indignation at what seemed to him to be mere nonsense. The idea that when the safety of the republic was thus at issue, when the control of an empire was to be determined by a few figures brought in by the telegraph, the leader, the man most deeply concerned, not merely for himself but for his country, could turn aside to read such balderdash and to laugh at such frivolous jests was, to his mind, repugnant, even damnable. He could not understand, apparently, that it was by the relief which these jests afforded to the strain of mind under which Lincoln had so long been living, and to the natural gloom of a melancholy and desponding temperament—

this was Mr. Lincoln's prevailing characteristic—that the safety and sanity of his intelligence were maintained and preserved.

"ON TO RICHMOND" AT LAST!

It was evident to all of us, as the spring of 1865 came on, that the war was drawing to a close. Sherman was coming northward from his triumphant march to the sea, and would soon be in communication with Grant, who, ever since I left him in July, 1864, had been watching Petersburg and Richmond, where Lee's army was shut up. At the end of March Grant advanced. On April 1st Sheridan won the battle of Five Forks; then on April 2d came the successful assaults which drove Lee from Petersburg.

On the morning of April 3d, before I had left my house, Mr. Stanton sent for me to come immediately to the War Department. When I reached his office, he told me that Richmond had surrendered, and that he wanted me to go down at once to report the condition of affairs. I started as soon as I could get a steamboat, Roscoe Conkling and my son Paul accompanying me. We arrived at City Point early on April 5th. Little was known there of the condition of things in Richmond. There were but a few officers left at the place, and those were overwhelmed with work. I had expected to find the President at City Point, he having been in the vicinity for several days, but Mr. Lincoln had gone up to Richmond the day before.

I started up the river immediately, and reached the town early in the afternoon. I went at once to find Major-General Godfrey Weitzel, who was in command of the United States forces. He was at his headquarters, which were in Jefferson Davis's former residence. I had heard down the river that Davis had sold his furniture at auction some days before the evacuation, but I found when I reached the house that this was a mistake—the furniture was all there.

Weitzel told me that he had learned at three o'clock in the morning of Monday, April 3d, that Richmond was being evacuated. He had moved forward at daylight, first taking care to give his men breakfast, in the expectation that they might have to fight. He met no opposition, and on entering the city was greeted with a hearty welcome from the mass of people. The mayor went out to meet him to surrender the city, but missed him on the road.

I took a walk around Richmond that day to see how much the city was injured. The Confederates in retreating had set it on fire, and the damage done in that way was enormous; nearly everything between Main Street and the river, for about three quarters of a mile, was burned. The custom house and the Spotswood Hotel were the only important buildings remaining in the burned district. The block opposite the Spotswood, including the Confederate War Department building, was entirely consumed. The Petersburg Railroad bridge, and that of the Danville road, were destroyed. All the enemy's vessels, excepting an unfinished ram which had her machinery in perfect order, were burned. The Tredegar Iron Works were unharmed. Libby Prison and Castle Thunder had also escaped the fire.

Immediately upon arriving I began to make inquiries about official papers. I found that the records and documents of the departments and of Congress had generally been removed before the evacuation, and that during the fire the Capitol had been ransacked and the documents there scattered. In the rooms of the Secretary of the Senate and of the Military Committee of the House of Representatives in the State House we found some papers of importance. They were in various cases in drawers, and all in great confusion. They were more or less imperfect and fragmentary. In the State Engineer's office also there were some boxes of papers relating to the Confederate works on the Potomac, around Norfolk, and on the Peninsula. I had all of these packed for shipment, without attempting to put them in order, and forwarded at once to Washington.

General Weitzel told me that he had found about twenty thousand people in Richmond, half of them of African descent. He said that when President Lincoln entered the town on the 4th he received a most enthusiastic reception from the mass of the inhabitants. All the members of Congress had escaped, and only the Assistant Secretary of War, Judge John Archibald Campbell, remained in the fallen capital of the Confederacy. Most of the newspaper editors had fled, but the Whig appeared on the 4th as a Union paper, with the name of its former proprietor at its head. The night after I arrived the theater opened.

There was much suffering and poverty among the population, the rich as well as the poor being destitute of food. Weitzel had decided to issue supplies to all who would take the oath. In my first message to Mr. Stanton I spoke of this. He immediately answered: "Please ascertain from General Weitzel under what authority he is distributing rations to the people of Richmond, as I suppose he would not do it without authority; and direct him to report daily the amount of rations distributed by his order to persons not belonging to the military service, and not authorized by law to receive rations, designating the color of the persons, their occupation, and sex." Mr. Stanton seemed to be satisfied when I wired him that Weitzel was working under General Ord's orders, approved by General Grant, and that he was paying for the rations by selling captured property.

The important question which the President had on his mind when I reached Richmond was how Virginia could be brought back to the Union. He had already had an interview with Judge Campbell and other prominent representatives of the Confederate Government. All they asked, they said, was an amnesty and a military convention to cover appearances. Slavery they admitted to be defunct. The President did not promise the amnesty, but he told them he had the pardoning power, and would save any repentant sinner from hanging. They assured him that, if amnesty could be offered, the rebel army would be dissolved and all the States return.

On the morning of the 7th, five members of the so-called Virginia Legislature held a meeting to consider written propositions which the President had handed to Judge Campbell. The President showed these papers to me confidentially. They were two in number. One stated reunion as a sine qua non; the second authorized General Weitzel to allow members of the body claiming to be the Legislature of Virginia to meet in Richmond for the purpose of recalling Virginia's soldiers from the rebel armies, with safe conduct to them so long as they did and said nothing hostile to the United States. In discussing with me these documents, the President remarked that Sheridan seemed to be getting rebel soldiers out of the war faster than the Legislature could think.

The next morning, on April 8th, I was present at an interesting interview between General Weitzel and General Shepley, who had been appointed as Military Governor of Richmond, and a committee of prominent citizens and members of the Legislature. Various papers were read by the Virginian representatives, but they were told plainly that no propositions could be entertained that involved a recognition of the Confederate authorities. The committee were also informed that if they desired to prepare an address to the people, advising them to abandon hostility to the Government at once, and begin to obey the laws of the United States, they should have every facility for its circulation through the State, provided, of course, that it met the approval of the military authorities. The two Union generals said that if the committee desired to call a convention of the prominent citizens of the State, with a view to the restoration of the authority of the United States Government, they would be allowed to go outside the lines of Richmond for the purpose of visiting citizens in different parts of the State and inducing them to take part in a convention. Safe conduct was promised to them for themselves and such citizens as they could persuade to attend the convention. They were also told that if they were not able to find conveyances for themselves for the journey into the country, horses would be loaned to them for that purpose. All this, they were informed, was not to be considered as in any manner condoning any offense of which any individual among them might have been guilty.

Judge Campbell said that he had no wish to take a prominent part in the proceedings, but that he had long since made up his mind that the cause of the South was hopeless. He had written a formal memorial to Jefferson Davis, immediately after the Hampton Roads conference, urging him and the Confederate

Congress to take immediate steps to stop the war and restore the Union. He had deliberately remained in Richmond to meet the consequences of his acts. He said that if he could be used in the restoration of peace and order, he would gladly undertake any labor that might be desired of him.

The spirit of the committee seemed to be generally the same as Judge Campbell's, though none of them equaled him in ability and clearness of thought and statement. They were thoroughly conscious that they were beaten, and sincerely anxious to stop all further bloodshed and restore peace, law, and order. This mental condition seemed to me to be very hopeful and encouraging.

One day, after the meeting of this committee, I was in the large room downstairs of the Spotswood Hotel when my name was called, and I turned around to see Andrew Johnson, the new Vice-President of the United States. He took me aside and spoke with great earnestness about the necessity of not taking the Confederates back without some conditions or without some punishment. He insisted that their sins had been enormous, and that if they were let back into the Union without any punishment the effect would be very bad. He said they might be very dangerous in the future. The Vice-President talked to me in this strain for fully twenty minutes, I should think. It was an impassioned, earnest speech that he made to me on the subject of punishing rebels. Finally, when he paused and I got a chance to reply, I said:

"Why, Mr. Johnson, I have no power in this case. Your remarks are very striking, very impressive, and certainly worthy of the most serious consideration, but it does not seem to me necessary that they should be addressed to me. They ought to be addressed to the President and to the members of Congress, to those who have authority in the case, and who will finally have to decide this question which you raise."

"Mr. Dana," said he, "I feel it to be my duty to say these things to every man whom I meet, whom I know to have any influence. Any man whose thoughts are considered by others, or whose judgment is going to weigh in the case, I must speak to, so that the weight of opinion in favor of the view of this question which I offer may possibly become preponderating and decisive.

That was in April. When Mr. Johnson became President, not long after, he soon came to take entirely the view which he condemned so earnestly in this conversation with me.

Toward the end of the first week after we entered Richmond the question about opening the churches on Sunday came up. I asked General Weitzel what he was going to do. He answered that all the places of worship were to be allowed to open on condition that no disloyalty should be uttered, and that the Episcopal clergymen should read the prayer for the President of the United States. But the next day General Shepley, the military governor, came to me to ask that the order might be relaxed so that the clergy should be required only not to pray for Davis. I declined giving any orders, having received none from Washington, and said that Weitzel must act in the matter entirely on his own judgment. Judge Campbell used all his influence with Weitzel and Shepley to get them to consent that a loyal prayer should not be exacted. Weitzel concluded not to give a positive order; his decision was influenced by the examples of New Orleans, Norfolk, and Savannah, where, he said, the requirement had not been at first enforced. In a greater measure, however, his decision was the result of the President's verbal direction to him to "let the people down easy." The churches were all well filled on Sunday, the ladies especially attending in great numbers. The sermons were devout and not political, the city was perfectly quiet, and there was more security for persons and property than had existed in Richmond for many months.

On Monday morning the news of Lee's surrender reached us in Richmond. It produced a deep impression. Even the most intensely partisan women now felt that the defeat was perfect and the rebellion finished, while among the men there was no sentiment but submission to the power of the nation, and a returning hope that their individual property might escape confiscation. They all seemed most keenly alive to this consideration, and men like General Anderson, the proprietor of the Tredegar works, were zealous in their efforts to produce a thorough pacification and save their possessions.

The next morning I received from Mr. Stanton an order to proceed to General Grant's headquarters and furnish from there such details as might be of interest. It was at this time that I had an interesting talk with Grant on the condition of Lee's army and about the men and arms surrendered. He told me that, in the long private interview which he had with Lee at Appomattox, the latter said that he should devote his whole efforts to pacifying the country and bringing the people back to the Union. Lee declared that he had always been for the Union in his own heart, and could find no justification for the politicians who had brought on the war, the origin of which he believed to have been in the folly of extremists on both sides. The war, Lee declared, had left him a poor man, with nothing but what he had upon his person, and his wife would have to provide for herself until he could find some employment.

The officers of Lee's army, Grant said, all seemed to be glad that it was over, and the men still more so than the officers. All were greatly impressed by the generosity of the terms finally granted to them, for at the time of the surrender they were surrounded and escape was impossible. General Grant thought that these terms were of great importance toward securing a thorough peace and undisturbed submission to the Government.

I returned to Washington with General Grant, reaching there the 13th, and taking up my work in the department at once.

THE CLOSING SCENES AT WASHINGTON

It was one of my duties at this time to receive the reports of the officers of the secret service in every part of the country. On the afternoon of the 14th of April—it was Good Friday—I got a telegram from the provost marshal in Portland, Me., saying: "I have positive information that Jacob Thompson will pass through Portland to-night, in order to take a steamer for England. What are your orders?"

Jacob Thompson, of Mississippi, had been Secretary of the Interior in President Buchanan's administration. He was a conspicuous secessionist, and for some time had been employed in Canada as a semi-diplomatic agent of the Confederate Government. He had been organizing all sorts of trouble and getting up raids, of which the notorious attack on St. Albans, Vt., was a specimen. I took the telegram and went down and read it to Mr. Stanton. His order was prompt: "Arrest him!" But as I was going out of the door he called to me and said: "No, wait; better go over and see the President."

At the White House all the work of the day was over, and I went into the President's business room without meeting any one. Opening the door, there seemed to be no one there, but, as I was turning to go out, Mr. Lincoln called to me from a little side room, where he was washing his hands:

"Halloo, Dana!" said he. "What is it? What's up?"

Then I read him the telegram from Portland.

"What does Stanton say?" he asked.

"He says arrest him, but that I should refer the question to you."

"Well," said the President slowly, wiping his hands, "no, I rather think not. When you have got an elephant by the hind leg, and he's trying to run away, it's best to let him run."

With this direction, I returned to the War Department.

"Well, what says he?" asked Mr. Stanton.

"He says that when you have got an elephant by the hind leg, and he is trying to run away, it's best to let him run."

"Oh, stuff!" said Stanton.

That night I was awakened from a sound sleep by a messenger with the news that Mr. Lincoln had been shot, and that the Secretary wanted me at a house in Tenth Street. I found the President with a bullet wound in the head, lying unconscious, though breathing heavily, on a bed in a small side room, while all the members of the Cabinet, and the Chief Justice with them, were gathered in the adjoining parlor. They seemed to be almost as much paralyzed as the unconscious sufferer within the little chamber. The surgeons said there was no hope. Mr. Stanton alone was in full activity.

"Sit down here" said he; "I want you."

Then he began and dictated orders, one after another, which I wrote out and sent swiftly to the telegraph. All these orders were designed to keep the business of the Government in full motion until the crisis should be over. It seemed as if Mr. Stanton thought of everything, and there was a great deal to be thought of that night. The extent of the conspiracy was, of course, unknown, and the horrible beginning which had been made naturally led us to suspect the worst. The safety of Washington must be looked after. Commanders all over the country had to be ordered to take extra precautions. The people must be notified of the tragedy. The assassins must be captured. The coolness and clear-headedness of Mr. Stanton under these circumstances were most remarkable. I remember that one of his first telegrams was to General Dix, the military commander of New York, notifying him of what had happened. No clearer brief account of the tragedy exists today than this, written scarcely three hours after the scene in Ford's Theater, on a little stand in the room where, a few feet away, Mr. Lincoln lay dying.

I remained with Mr. Stanton until perhaps three o'clock in the morning. Then he said: "That's enough. Now you may go home."

When I left, the President was still alive, breathing heavily and regularly, though, of course, quite unconscious. About eight o'clock I was awakened by a rapping on a lower window. It was Colonel Pelouze, of the adjutant-general's office, and he said:

"Mr. Dana, the President is dead, and Mr. Stanton directs you to arrest Jacob Thompson."

The order was sent to Portland, but Thompson couldn't be found there. He had taken the Canadian route to Halifax.

The whole machinery of the War Department was now employed in the effort to secure the murderer of the President and his accomplices. As soon as I had recovered from the first shock of Mr. Lincoln's death, I remembered that in the previous November I had received from General Dix the following letter:

Headquarters, Department of the East,

New York City, November 17, 1864.

C. A. Dana, Esq.

My dear Sir: The inclosed was picked up in a Third Avenue railroad car. I should have thought the whole thing got up for the Sunday Mercury but for the genuine letter from St. Louis in a female hand. The Charles Selby is obviously a manufacture. The party who dropped the letter was heard to say he would start for Washington Friday night. He is of medium size, has black hair and whiskers, but the latter are believed to be a disguise. He had disappeared before the letter was picked up and examined.

Yours truly,

John A. Dix.

There were two inclosures, this being one of them:

Dear Louis: The time has at last come that we have all so wished for, and upon you everything depends. As it was decided before you left, we were to cast lots. Accordingly we did so, and you are to be the Charlotte Corday of the nineteenth century. When you remember the fearful, solemn vow that was taken by us, you will feel there is no drawback—Abe must die, and now. You can choose your weapons. The cup, the knife, the bullet. The cup failed us once, and might again. Johnson, who will give this, has been like an enraged demon since the meeting, because it has not fallen upon him to rid the world of the monster. He says the blood of his gray-haired father and his noble brother call upon him for revenge, and revenge he will have; if he cannot wreak it upon the fountain-head, he will upon some of the bloodthirsty generals. Butler would suit him. As our plans were all concocted and well arranged, we separated, and as I am writing—on my way to Detroit—I will only say that all rests upon you. You know where to find your friends. Your disguises are so perfect and complete that without one knew your face no police telegraphic dispatch would catch you. The English gentleman "Harcourt" must not act hastily. Remember he has ten days. Strike for your home, strike for your country; bide your time, but strike sure. Get introduced, congratulate him, listen to his stories—not many more will the brute tell to earthly friends. Do anything but fail, and meet us at the appointed place within the fortnight. Inclose this note, together with one of poor Leenea. I will give the reason for this when we meet. Return by Johnson. I wish I could go to you, but duty calls me to the West; you will probably hear from me in Washington. Sanders is doing us no good in Canada.

Believe me, your brother in love,

Charles Selby.

The other was in a woman's handwriting:

St. Louis, October 21, 1864.

Dearest Husband: Why do you not come home? You left me for ten days only, and you now have been from home more than two weeks. In that long time only sent me one short note—a few cold words—and a check for money, which I did not require. What has come over you? Have you forgotten your wife and child? Baby calls for papa until my heart aches. We are so lonely without you. I have written to you again and again, and, as a last resource, yesterday wrote to Charlie, begging him to see you and tell you to come home. I am so ill, not able to leave my room; if I was, I would go to you wherever you were, if in this world. Mamma says I must not write any more, as I am too weak. Louis, darling, do not stay away any longer from your heart-broken wife.

Leenea.

On reading the letters, I had taken them at once to President Lincoln. He looked at them, but made no special remark, and, in fact, seemed to attach very little importance to them. I left them with him.

I now reminded Mr. Stanton of this circumstance, and he asked me to go immediately to the White House and see if I could find the letters. I thought it rather doubtful, for I knew the President received a great many communications of a similar nature. However, I went over, and made a thorough search through his private desk. He seemed to have attached more importance to these papers than to others of the kind, for I found them inclosed in an envelope marked in his own handwriting, "Assassination." I kept the letters by me for some time, and then delivered them to Judge John A. Bingham, special judge advocate in the conspiracy trial. Judge Bingham seemed to think them of importance, and asked me to have General Dix send the finder down to Washington. I wired at once to the general. He replied that it was a woman who had found the letters; that she was keeping a small store in New York, had several children, was a widow, and had no servant; that she would have to find someone to take care of her house, but would be in Washington in a day or two.

A few days later she came. I was not in town when Mrs. Hudspeth, as her name proved to be, arrived. I had gone to Chicago, but from the woman's testimony on May 12th, I learned that in November, 1864, just after the presidential election, and on the day, she said, on which General Butler left New York, she had overheard a curious conversation between two men in a Third Avenue car in New York city. She had observed, when a jolt of the car pushed the hat of one of the men forward, that he wore false whiskers. She had noticed that his hand was very beautiful; that he carried a pistol in his belt; that, judging from his conversation, he was a young man of education; she heard him say that he was going to Washington that day. The young men left the car before she did, and after they had gone her daughter, who was with her, had picked up a letter from the floor. Mrs. Hudspeth, thinking it belonged to her, had carried it from the car.

She afterward discovered the two letters printed above, and took them to General Scott, who, upon reading them, said they were of great importance, and sent her to General Dix. When a photograph of Booth was shown to Mrs. Hudspeth, she swore that it was the man in disguise whom she had seen in the car. It was found that Booth was in New York on the day that she indicated—that is, the day General Butler left New York, November 11th—and likewise that Booth had gone from there to Washington, as she had heard this man say he was going to do. The inference was that the man who had dropped the letter was Booth.

I was afterward called to the stand, on June 9th, to testify about the letters. Judge Bingham used these documents as a link in his chain of evidence showing that a conspiracy existed "to kill and murder Abraham Lincoln, William H. Seward, Andrew Johnson, Ulysses S. Grant, Edwin M. Stanton, and others of his advisers," and that Booth was a partner in this conspiracy.

I have said that I was in Chicago when Mrs. Hudspeth gave her testimony. Just after I reached there I received from Major T. F. Eckert, the head of the military telegraph, a message saying that the court wanted me immediately as a witness in the conspiracy trial. I returned at once, and on the 18th of May appeared in court. I was wanted that I might testify to the identity of a key to a secret cipher which I had found on the 6th of April in Richmond. On that day I had gone into the office of Mr. Benjamin, the Confederate Secretary of State; on a shelf, among Mr. Benjamin's books and other things, I had found a secret cipher key. I saw it was the key to the official Confederate cipher, and, as we had at times to decipher at the War Department a good many documents written in that cipher, it seemed to me of interest, and I brought it away, with several other interesting documents. When I returned to Washington I gave it to Major Eckert, who had charge of cipher dispatches in the War Department.

The secret cipher key was a model consisting of a cylinder, six inches in length and two and one half in diameter, fixed in a frame, the cylinder having the printed key pasted over it. By shifting the pointers fixed over the cylinder on the upper portion of the frame, according to a certain arrangement previously agreed upon, the cipher letter or dispatch could be deciphered readily. The model was put in evidence at the trial.—note in original

Now, on the night of Mr. Lincoln's assassination, Lieutenant W. H. Terry had been sent to the National Hotel to seize the trunk of J. Wilkes Booth. Among other things, he had found a paper containing a secret cipher. When this was given to Major Eckert, he immediately saw that it was the same as the one which I had found in Richmond. It was thought that possibly by means of this evidence it could be shown that Booth was in communication with the Confederate Government. I was called back to identify the cipher key. Major Eckert at the same time presented dispatches written in the cipher found in Booth's trunk and sent from Canada to the Confederates. They had been captured and taken to the War Department, where copies of them were made. By the key which I had found these dispatches could be read. These dispatches indicated plots against the leaders of our Government, though whether Booth had sent them or not was, of course, never known.

Throughout the period of the trial I was constantly receiving and answering messages and letters relative to the examination or arrest of persons suspected of being connected with the affair. In most cases neither the examinations nor arrests led to anything. The persons had been acquaintances of the known conspirators, or they had been heard to utter disloyal sentiments and had been reported to the department by zealous Unionists. It was necessary, however, under the circumstances, to follow up every clew given us, and, under Mr. Stanton's directions, I gave attention to all cases reported.

While the trial was going on in Washington, Jefferson Davis was captured, on May 10th, near Irwinsville, Ga., by a detachment of General Wilson's cavalry. Mr. Davis and his family, with Alexander H. Stephens, lately Vice-President of the Confederacy, John II. Reagan, Postmaster General, Clement C. Clay, and other State prisoners, were sent to Fortress Monroe. The propeller

Clyde, with the party on board, reached Hampton Roads on May 19th. The next day, May 20th, Mr. Stanton sent for me to come to his office. He told me where Davis was, and said that he had ordered General Nelson A. Miles to go to Hampton Roads to take charge of the prisoners, transferring them from the Clyde to the fortress. Mr. Stanton was much concerned lest Davis should commit suicide; he said that he himself would do so in like circumstances. "I want you to go to Fortress Monroe," he said, "and caution General Miles against leaving Davis any possible method of suicide; tell him to put him in fetters, if necessary. Davis must be brought to trial; he must not be allowed to kill himself." Mr. Stanton also told me that he wanted a representative of the War Department down there to see what the military was doing, and to give suggestions and make criticisms and send him full reports.

The status of Jefferson Davis at the time explains Mr. Stanton's anxiety. It should be remembered that Davis had not surrendered when the capital of the Confederacy, Richmond, was captured; neither had he surrendered with either of the two principal armies under Lee and Johnston. At that time the whole Confederate army west of the Mississippi was still at large. To allow Davis to join this force was only to give the Confederacy an opportunity to reassemble the forces still unsurrendered and make another stand for life. Even more important than this consideration was the fact that Davis was charged, in President Johnson's proclamation of May 2, 1865, offering a reward for his capture, with instigating the assassination of President Lincoln:

> Whereas, It appears, from evidence in the Bureau of Military Justice, that the atrocious murder of the late President, Abraham Lincoln, and the attempted assassination of the Hon. W. H. Seward, Secretary of State, were incited, concerted, and procured by and between Jefferson Davis, late of Richmond, Va., . . . and other rebels and traitors against the Government of the United States, harbored in Canada;
>
> Now, therefore, to the end that justice may be done, I, Andrew Johnson, President of the United States, do offer and promise for the arrest of said persons or either of them, within the limits of the

United States, so that they can be brought to trial, the following rewards: One hundred thousand dollars for the arrest of Jefferson Davis . . . The provost marshal general of the United States is directed to cause the descriptions of said persons, with notice of the above rewards, to be published.

It was with the above facts in mind that I started for Hampton Roads on May 20th. On the 22d the prisoners were transferred from the Clyde to the fortress. The quarter selected for Davis's prison was a casemate such as at that time, as well as at the present, is occupied by officers and their families. In fact, an officer with his family was moved out of the particular casemate in which Davis was placed. Anyone who will take the trouble to visit Fortress Monroe can see the place still, and it certainly has not today a gloomy or forbidding appearance. The whole scene of the transfer I described in a long telegram which I sent to Mr. Stanton on the 22d. As it contains my fresh impressions, and has never before been published, I give it here in full:

From Fortress Monroe,

1 p. m., May 22, 1865.

Hon. E. M. Stanton, Secretary of War:

The two prisoners have just been placed in their respective casemates. The sentries are stationed both within and without their doors. The bars and locks are fastened, and the regular routine of their imprisonment has begun. At precisely one o'clock General Miles left with a tug and a guard from the garrison to go for Davis and Clay. At half past one the tug left the Clyde for the fortress. She landed at the engineers' wharf, and the procession, led by the cavalrymen of Colonel Pritchard's command, moved through the water battery on the east front of the fortress and entered by a postern leading from that battery. The cavalrymen were followed by General Miles, holding Davis by the right arm. Next came half a dozen soldiers, and then Colonel Pritchard with Clay, and last the guard which Miles took out with him. The arrangements were excellent and successful, and not a single curious spectator was anywhere in sight.

Davis bore himself with a haughty attitude. His face was somewhat flushed, but his features were com- posed and his step firm. In Clay's manner there was less expression of bravado and dramatic determination. Both were dressed in gray, with drab slouched hats. Davis wore a thin dark overcoat. His hair and beard are not so gray as has been reported, and he seems very much less worn and broken by anxiety and labor than Mr. Blair reported when he returned from Richmond last winter. The parties were not informed that they were not to be removed to the fortress until General Miles went on board the Clyde, but they had before learned generally what was their destination.

From his staff officers Davis parted yesterday, shedding tears at the separation. The same scene has just been renewed at his parting from Harrison, his private secretary, who left at one o'clock for Washington. In leaving his wife and children he exhibited no great emotion, though she was violently affected. He told her she would be allowed to see him in the course of the day. Clay took leave of his wife in private, and he was not seen by the officers. Both asked to see General Halleck, but he will not see them.

The arrangements for the security of the prisoners seem to me as complete as could be desired. Each one occupies the inner room of a casemate; the window is heavily barred. A sentry stands within, before each of the doors leading into the outer room. These doors are to be grated, but are now secured by bars fastened on the outside. Two other sentries stand outside of these doors. An officer is also constantly on duty in ' the outer room, whose duty is to see his prisoners every fifteen minutes. The outer door of all is locked on the outside, and the key is kept exclusively by the general officer of the guard. Two sentries are also stationed without that door, and a strong line of sentries cuts off all access to the vicinity of the casemates. Another line is stationed on the top of the parapet overhead, and a third line is posted across the moats on the counterscarps opposite the places of confinement. The casemates on each side and between these occupied by the prisoners are used as guard rooms, and soldiers are always there. A lamp is constantly kept burning in each of the rooms. The furniture of each prisoner is a hospital bed, with iron bedstead, chair and table, and a movable stool closet. A Bible is allowed to each. I have not given orders to have them placed in irons, as General Halleck seemed opposed to it, but General Miles is instructed to have fetters ready if he thinks them necessary. The prisoners are to be supplied with soldiers' rations, cooked by the guard. Their linen will be issued to them in the same way. I shall be back tomorrow morning.

C. A. Dana.

Before leaving Fortress Monroe, on May 22d, I made out for General Miles...[an] order ... for placing fetters upon Davis a day or two later, when he found it necessary to change the inner doors of the casemate, which were light wooden ones, without locks. While these doors were being changed for grated ones, anklets were placed on Davis; they did not prevent his walking, but did prevent any attempt to jump past the guard, and they also prevented him from running. As soon as the doors were changed (it required three days, I think), the anklets were removed. I believe that every care was taken during Mr. Davis's imprisonment to remove cause for complaint. Medical officers were directed to superintend his meals and give him everything that would excite his appetite. As it was complained that his quarters in the casemate were unhealthy and disagreeable, he was, after a few weeks, transferred to Carroll Hall, a building still occupied by officers and soldiers. That Davis's health was not ruined by his imprisonment at Fortress Monroe is proved by the fact that he came out of the prison in better condition than when he went in, and that he lived for twenty years afterward, and died of old age.

I hurried back to Washington from Fortress Monroe to be present at the grand review of the Armies of the Potomac and Tennessee, which had been arranged for May 23d and 24th. I reached the city early in the morning. The streets were all alive with detachments of soldiers marching toward Capitol Hill, for it was there that the parade was to start. Thousands of visitors were also in the streets.

May 23d was given up to the review of the Army of the Potomac, and by nine o'clock General Meade and his staff, at the head of the army, started from the Capitol. Soon after, I joined the company on the reviewing officers' stand, in front of the White House, in just the place which the reviewing stand now occupies on inauguration days. President Johnson had the central position on the platform. Upon his right, a seat was retained for the commander of the corps undergoing review. As soon as the corps commander with his staff had passed the grand stand at the head of his troops, he rode into the grounds of the White House, dismounted, and came to take his position at the right of Mr. Johnson, while his troops continued their march. When all his men had passed, he gave up his place to the commander of the next corps in the column, and so on. Next to the corps commanders were seated Secretary Stanton and Lieutenant-General Grant. On the left of the President was Postmaster-General Dennison and, on the first day of the parade, while the Army of the Potomac passed, Major-General Meade; and on the second day, while the Army of the Tennessee passed, Major-General Sherman. The other members of the Cabinet, many army officers, the assistant secretaries in the different departments, and a number of guests invited by the President and the secretaries, were grouped around these central personages.

On the 24th, when Sherman's army was reviewed, I sat directly behind Mr. Stanton at the moment when General Sherman, after having passed the grand stand at the head of his army, dismounted and came on to the stand to take his position and review his soldiers.

As he had to pass immediately in front of Secretary Stanton in order to reach the place assigned to him on the President's right, I could see him perfectly. I watched both men closely, for the difficulty between Stanton and Sherman was at that moment known to everybody.

The terms upon which Sherman in April had accepted the surrender of General Joseph E. Johnston's army in North Carolina went beyond the authority of a military commander, and touched upon political issues. It is true that these terms were made conditional upon the approval of the Government; nevertheless, Mr. Stanton was deeply indignant at the general for meddling with matters beyond his jurisdiction. No doubt his indignation was intensified by his dislike of Sherman. The two men were antagonistic by nature. Sherman was an effervescent, mercurial, expansive man, springing abruptly to an idea, expressing himself enthusiastically on every subject, and often without reflection. Stanton could not accommodate himself to this temperament.

When the memorandum of the agreement between Johnston and Sherman reached Stanton, he sent Grant to the general in hot haste, and then published in the newspapers, which need not have known anything of the affair, a full account of the unwise compact, and an indignant repudiation of it by the Government. Naturally this brought down a furious attack upon Sherman. All his past services were forgotten for a time, and he was even called a "traitor." The public quickly saw the injustice of this attitude; so did most of the men in the Government, and they hastened to appease Sherman, who was violently incensed over what he called Stanton's insult. I think he never forgave the Secretary. When, on May 19th, he reached Washington with his army, which he had marched northward across the battlefields of Virginia, he refused to have anything to do with Stanton, although Grant tried his best to bring about a reconciliation and the President and several members of the Cabinet showed him every attention.

I was, of course, curious to see what General Sherman would do in passing before Mr. Stanton to take his place on the stand. The general says in his *Memoirs* that, as he passed, Stanton offered his hand and he refused to take it. He is entirely mistaken. I was watching narrowly. The Secretary made no motion to offer his hand, or to exchange salutations in any manner. As the general passed, Mr. Stanton gave him merely a slight forward motion of his head, equivalent, perhaps, to a quarter of a bow.

In May I had been asked to become the editor of a new paper to be founded in Chicago, the *Republican*. The active promoter was a Mr. Mack, and the concern was organized with a nominal capital of five hundred thousand dollars. Only a small part of this was ever paid up; a large block of the stock was set aside as a bonus to induce a proper man to become the editor. Mr. Mack had offered the post to me, and, through the influence of the Hon. Lyman Trumbull [Senator and co-author of the Thirteenth

Amendment] and other prominent men of Illinois, I was persuaded to accept it. In deciding on the change, I had arranged to stay in Washington until I could finish the routine business upon which I was then engaged, and until Mr. Stanton could conveniently spare me. This was not until the 1st of July. On the first day of the month I sent to the President my resignation as Assistant Secretary of War, and a few days later I left the capital for Chicago.

THE END

DISCOVER MORE LOST HISTORY AT <u>BIGBYTEBOOKS.COM</u>

Made in United States
North Haven, CT
30 December 2021